THE BEST
AUSTRALIAN
POEMS
2009

THE BEST AUSTRALIAN POEMS 2009

Edited by
ROBERT ADAMSON

Published by Black Inc.,
an imprint of Schwartz Media Pty Ltd

Level 5, 289 Flinders Lane
Melbourne Victoria 3000 Australia
email: enquiries@blackincbooks.com
http://www.blackincbooks.com

Introduction and this collection
© Robert Adamson & Black Inc., 2009.
Individual poems © retained by the authors.

Every effort has been made to contact the copyright
holders of material in this book. However where
an omission has occurred, the publisher will gladly
include acknowledgment in any future edition.

ALL RIGHTS RESERVED.
No part of this publication may be reproduced, stored
in a retrieval system, or transmitted in any form or
by any means electronic, mechanical, photocopying,
recording or otherwise without the prior consent
of the publishers.

ISBN 9781863954525

Printed in Australia by Griffin Press

Contents

Robert Adamson Introduction xi

* * *

Martin Harrison Word 1

Adam Aitken Pol Pot in Paris 3
Ivy Alvarez Curing the animal 5
Mandy Beaumont We Are Standing 6
Sarah K. Bell reconstructing a rabbit 9
Judith Beveridge Rain 11
Judith Bishop In the Somme 13
Ken Bolton Outdoor Pig-keeping, 1954 & My Other Books on Farming Pigs 14
Michael Brennan After Fred Williams' *You Yangs 1* 17
David Brooks A Place on Earth 19
  Ninox strenua 21
Jen Jewel Brown breath 22
Pam Brown Blue Glow 24
joanne burns harbinger 29
Larry Buttrose London Fields 32
Michelle Cahill After the Headlines 34

Elizabeth Campbell	Ithaka 35
Ali Cobby Eckermann	Intervention Pay Back 37
Stuart Cooke	North Durras Caravan Park 42
Shevaun Cooley	Expeditions with W.G. Sebald 45
Luke Davies	Maldon, 991 A.D. 49
Sarah Day	A Dry Winter: Some Observations About Rain 50
Lucy Dougan	The Ties My Sister Makes 53
Laurie Duggan	Letter to John Forbes 54
Adrienne Eberhard	The Maze 56
Stephen Edgar	Murray Dreaming 58
Chris Edwards	The Big Splash 60
Anne Elvey	Between 61
Kate Fagan	From *The Correspondence* 62
Jeltje Fanoy	Surfers Paradise (Qld)/ Reporting for the Night Watch 64
Michael Farrell	muzak to view the city with 66
Susan Fealy	Notes on Art and Dying: 19.10.2008 … *How to paint a rose* 67
Johanna Featherstone	Mother Looking into Her Son's Bedroom 68
Jayne Fenton Keane	The Boot Left in the Snow 69
Claire Gaskin	Exile 71
Jane Gibian	Sound Piece 75

Lisa Gorton	A Description of the Storm Glass and Guide to Its Use in Forecasting Weather 77
Robert Gray	Classifying the Animals 79
Jennifer Harrison	Kakadu 80
Martin Harrison	Wallabies 82
J.S. Harry	Braid on Braid 86
Kevin Hart	Dark Bird 89
Susan Hawthorne	Climate change: *yugantameghaha* 90
Matt Hetherington	The words in brackets are from Gaskin's 'A Bud' 91
Barry Hill	Egret 94
	Waking Happens in Reservoirs 95
Lia Hills	an anatomy of birds 96
Sarah Holland-Batt	Capriccio: Spring 97
L.K. Holt	For Nina 100
Clive James	*Meteor IV* at Cowes, 1913 102
Carol Jenkins	When Years Take the Stars Away 104
A. Frances Johnson	Black Cockatoo: *Calyptorhynchus funereus* 105
	The Wind-up Birdman of Moorabool Street 106
Jill Jones	Oh, Sydney 107
Amanda Joy	Chased Seas Urge 109
Paul Kelly	Thoughts in the Middle of the Night 110

Paul Kelly	One More Tune 111
Anthony Lawrence	Leonard Cohen in Concert, Hunter Valley, January 2009 112
	The Burden & the Wing 114
Michelle Leber	Heat Wave, Melbourne– Hottest Day on Record since 1855 118
Geoffrey Lehmann	The Animals 120
John Leonard	Rain in March 122
Kerry Leves	'We believe in killing idiots' 124
Debbie Lim	The Egret 126
Astrid Lorange	Fred's Farm 128
Rose Lucas	Even in the Dark 129
Kent MacCarter	Twenty-five Unbroken Bottles of Champ 130
Jennifer Maiden	Clare and Paris 132
David McCooey	Memory & Slaughter 136
Susan McCreery	Rock Fishing 141
Kate Middleton	To Peter Rabbit in the Night 142
Peter Minter	The Latter Shall Prevail 143
Meg Mooney	Birdwatching during the Intervention 146
Derek Motion	hush 148
Les Murray	Port Jackson Greaseproof Rose 149
David Musgrave	Phantom Limb 151

Jenni Nixon	A Bombardier on the Bus	152
Jan Owen	Climbing the Nectarine Tree at Dusk	154
Geoff Page	Richard Rorty (1931–2007)	156
π.O.	'Mo' McCackie 1892–1953	159
Felicity Plunkett	Venery	161
Dorothy Porter	Travel	162
Peter Porter	After Schiller	164
Ron Pretty	Kate Dancing	165
Peter Rose	Morbid Transfers	167
Robyn Rowland	Is the light right?	170
Gig Ryan	Tormented Syllogism Held at Bay	171
Philip Salom	Reading Francis Webb	173
Jaya Savige	The Pain Switch	174
Berndt Sellheim	Necromantic	175
Thomas Shapcott	Monteverdi at 74	177
Craig Sherborne	Slipper	180
Alex Skovron	Lives	181
Andrew Slattery	Triptych	183
Vivian Smith	In the Butterfly House, Vienna	184
Alicia Sometimes	This Machine Kills Fascists	185
Maria Takolander	Anaesthetic	188
Tim Thorne	Cimitière Marin Revisited	190
Jessika Tong	The Light Went Off in Me	195

John Tranter	The Anaglyph 196
Mark Tredinnick	Improvisations on a Daylight Moon 206
Chris Wallace-Crabbe	Torture is a Dirty Word 208
Louise Waller	Three Rivers Triptych 210
John Watson	Four Ways to Approach the Numinous 212
Meredith Wattison	Holbein Through Silk 220
Alan Wearne	Dysfunction, North Carlton Style or The Widow of Noosa 221
Petra White	The Orchardist 227
Fiona Wright	Kinglake 228
Fay Zwicky	Pages 230

PUBLICATION DETAILS
233

Introduction

Soul clap its hands and sing, and louder sing. —W.B. YEATS

When Yeats uses the word 'soul', it feels tangible. There's a bird in a poem by Gerard Manley Hopkins, the woodlark, whose song goes: 'Teevo cheevo cheevio chee, Weedio-weedio'. This delightful song inspires the poet to answer: 'Sweet, of a sweet, of a sweet joy / Of a sweet – a sweet – sweet – joy'. When Meg Mooney hears birds in Central Australia, orange-beaked finches, they chatter urgently in Pitjantjatjara: 'Nyii-nyi, nyii-nyi, nyii-nyi'. Through these songs we can hear two poets, one in the 1880s in Ireland and the other at the bottom of the world in 2008, singing through time and space. There are many birds and lyrics in this anthology, the poets sing to each other and their poems set words dancing in our souls.

I have been reading the poems for twelve months, at first clipping whatever caught my fancy, making piles that became my shortlists. I managed to read all the poetry in the print publications as well as many of the electronic journals and even blogs that feature poems. Then came the monthly bundles of submissions that my editor, Adam Shaw, sent on from Black Inc. to my post box. By July the piles of poetry had taken over my study and had started to creep out into the rest of the house. I read thousands of poems before I managed to select the 102 poets that made the final cut. I'm sure many good poems slipped through the net and I apologise to the poets that I may have missed. I managed to convince Black Inc. to extend the number of pages to accommodate the embarrassment of riches that I came up with in the end. I am truly excited by the poetry I have collected here. So perhaps it is enough to say that I am not going to take up too much space by reviewing specific poems. I would rather let the poems speak for themselves.

I wanted this book to be a fairly inclusive survey of the 'best' poetry written in Australia in the last year and to represent some of the younger poets I discovered in my reading. What kept me excited was the exuberance in the language and ideas of poets whose names I hardly knew, and whose work started to threaten to take over the space reserved for those whose poetry I have been following for many years. In the end I managed to represent quite a few young poets, though not as well as I would have liked. I hope there's enough of this new work to indicate to readers the power of the in-coming tide – there's nothing as rewarding as discovering a new poet, someone who has managed to come up with a voice that has a trace of the authentic about it. Not such an easy thing; it takes courage to be yourself, to write the poem about what you actually believe. This has to involve an ability to craft the language of the heart or soul into the right form. Such a poet has to know well the traditions from which they learn their skill in order to re-imagine and rewrite them in a new way.

I remember reading an anthology in the late 1960s. The editor published a startling statement by Francis Webb about the state of Australian poetry at the time. Here's the last sentence: 'The tried and tested poets are perfecting clear communication; and some of the younger are turning to experiment and a conscious widening of frontiers – healthy indeed, provided that we are not infected by that ancient disease, iconoclasm.' This was rather shocking to me at the time because I admired Webb's poetry tremendously, and yet I was very much under the influence of Ezra Pound's modernism and was attempting to follow his catch-cry and 'make it new'. I think because Webb's phrase, 'that ancient disease, iconoclasm', is such a well-made one, it resonated in my imagination and somehow influenced the kind of poetry I wrote.

When Australian poetry soars to new heights, it's usually because poets open up to the whole place. Ignoring current fashions, they take risks and write from the core of our culture. This is what Michael Dransfield meant when he said that 'poets are the salt of the earth'. When our poetry seems interesting, sleek and sharp, it's because poets write what is often a highly self-conscious version of what's happening in New York or London. The deep tradition is the one that is reflected in the work of poets such as Randolph Stow, Judith Wright, Roland Robinson and Francis Webb. There are some writers in this anthology who are opening their work up to this tradition by writing about their lives in the poetry of witness.

I attended the APC Regional Poetry Festival at Castlemaine in April 2008. Ali Cobby Eckermann, a poet from Alice Springs, was on the program and she read a poem I have included here, 'Intervention Pay Back'. Ali recited this poem and the audience was clearly moved. I was certainly moved by both the subject matter and the language of the poem. Somewhere between a ballad and written spoken word, it makes a new shift into what a poem might say or be.

I accepted a poem by John Tranter early in the process of editing; long and postmodern, it acted as a sort of counter-balance. I had to find another strong, lengthy poem in a different style for variety. I found Ali's intervention poem in a manuscript she submitted and it sat somewhere near the front of this anthology, and as the poems were in alphabetical order, Tranter's poem was toward the end. Longer poems came in and I accepted a few. I could easily have edited an anthology of the long poem, but I wanted to create a rhythm for the reader: shorter lyrics and some satirical poems, then hopefully a few love poems, poems of weather, landscape poems and, of course, bird poems.

People ask me, why are so many bird poems being written and published? I have a theory: we miss having poets among us who can imagine that a soul can 'clap its hands and sing, and louder sing', that we need to acknowledge visitations by intense psychological presences, and that birds are the closest things we have, more or less, to angels.

It wasn't until I compiled the index that I noticed there were more women poets than men in this year's anthology. It is the first time there has been a gender balance where the scales have tipped in favour of women in this series: it has turned out to be the year of the women poets.

Last year we lost one of our finest poets. Dorothy Porter died, aged fifty-four, on 10 December 2008. I have included her poem 'Travel' in this anthology, and in memory of her I have placed Martin Harrison's poem 'Word' at the front of the book.

Robert Adamson
Hawkesbury River

Word

i.m. Dorothy Porter

Warm river-wind offers its rocking-horse rhythm
to the tired barge and its ancient melody
and the melody of film and o so subtle detection
in which briefly suddenly one voice's glimmer is lost
how old how birdlike she had made it how ancient
the light tracery of clip and scene   Like some
transparent frame in a mystery-tale whose truth's murder
(cruel innocence of all our inevitable deaths)
a life's spent searching for the phrase perhaps
best sung – innocence of springtime springtime –
by those performers who exquisitely come on stage
always at one remove from more than possible truth
o what a life in words o how much quiet light
in those young rooms back then by the harbour
which could have sheltered us eternally in the value
of sweet speech ignoring the plot's speed so what's in a

Martin Harrison

Pol Pot in Paris

Oh happy child, kindly teacher – were you a fake?
Like you I'm taciturn
but when I give an order who's to hear?
Paris, I found it cold but didn't read very much.
No one knows what you thought of its weather,
the river, the churches or the metro.
You preferred a book on the Soviets to girls in Montmartre.
I too would rather recite Verlaine
than take notes on electronics.
If I had a history and traditions, I don't remember.
Would you understand me?
I too lived on an allowance
of uncomfortable epithets
cobbled from Buddha and Marx:
'Physical beauty is an obstacle to the will to struggle.'

Late nights drinking weren't your thing.
Sweet words of girls 'mask evil hearts'.
A fun holiday on a tractor in Belgrade.
'The wheels of revolution never stop, roll on
to crush all who dare to walk in its path.'
We could have been lifetime friends, together
rooting out evil, picking mushrooms,
sipping coffee in the Latin Quarter,
mediocre, polite, soft spoken
migrants meandering in overcoats.

The others marry French girls, you join a work brigade
digging ditches in Zagreb.
In the 15th arrondissement, Rue Latellier
mid-winter, dog shit everywhere.

On the river it's 20 francs
for *La Grande Révolution Française*.
We could've talked, taken notes for a memoir:
did you join the party before or after the festival
in East Berlin? Did you buy that shirt
before or after the coup d'état?

In Marseille you boarded the *Jamaïque*.
Your tiny shadow cast a conspiracy
of epic dimensions, and there, in the oily backwash
and the silver wake, a complete solution.
I too went home, dreaming of a family
I would never have, and the one I would.

Adam Aitken

Curing the animal

My husband hands me the animal.
A soft neck roll and a dead eye,
a lustreless fur that I must touch
to strip and salt and peg to dry.
He is away all the day in the dust.
a eucalypt oil smell taints his neck
he comes to me
bones meeting mine
a hard fit
a green lawn at the edge of a desert
my heart, inexact
There is a sharp knife in the house.
I gather the wattle bark and boil it in a drum,
leave the skin to reek and call flies to it.
weeks pass, his eyes squint with distance,
monosyllables doled out, hard shillings
minted rare from his mouth, whiskers on his chin
scratch my skin. I pretend. Sleep.
Pulling one parsnip each, one leek.
The hard-fought cream, the butter's luxury.
The wallaby seasons its last useful night,
salt and pepper crusts its meat, the oil rolling
like mist off a morning.
Brown and sere of fat, it rests.
The marjoram rubs its scent on me.
The leek becomes soft, the parsnip tender
under butter. The meat drowns in gravy.
He chews 'til all the flesh is gone.
I pull the reddish hide from the reeking drum,
tip water to thirsty ground,
watch it drain.

Ivy Alvarez

We Are Standing

We are standing still,
so very still
under the pale whites of
this summer moon.

It grabs at every
feature on our faces
and pulls them upwards.
Making our shadows ominous,
almost religious
in its stillness.

Pale whites

We have driven for hours
to this
our new home.
The land we
have just marked as our own,
by looking only at small photographs
and talking on our phones
to a man named Jonathon
for months,
months of placing all our bets on
the splendid dream.

And here we are
forty miles
from any
nearby town,
ground solid beneath our feet.
Where our day has turned into
our night,
and we stand looking out at her.
Our new –
Everything.

And she welcomes us
in her long grassed
honesty.
Unfurling towards us
a mass of hills
and silver soaked trees,
breaking through
the darkness of the night sky's
trembling
black
blue
walls.

She could wake dreamers and split hearts with her night beauty

She surrounds us with her biography.
What she has seen
before our births and
those of our fathers.
And she steadies our feet to the spot,
fixing us
to
her grace
mother like lines.

And we stand
fold into each other's
white skins.
Skins that have not seen the light of day
in the city living we have so
become tired of
involved with
drunk in the rush of it all.

We fold
sew our hands together.
Mouths soft from her
and
kiss.

Losing all the years
between
the day we first met.
Where once,
the only thing between us was
cotton candy tastes on lips
and the promise
of our great love
floating like balloons
over street corners.

And tonight,
here
with our
everything

we are lost in this
now
forever.

Mandy Beaumont

reconstructing a rabbit

take something sharp
& begin

    observe

the crescent curve of his back
folded fullmoon   the rabbit world opens
    thickly; darkly bound these stitches

        you are bookbinder   cartographer
        historian: this body of work to be studied

the rabbit measures by its teeth
where all wisdom is stored   how it discovers
its existence   identity
    kit & kindle
        its rabbit-proof

remove the incisors   these are your luck
the feet may be soft & more sightly
    yes, but they are
    merely decoration

knowledge is the greater fortune

    ask the rabbit on the tall ship
    the rabbit with the pocketwatch

    (((((

the ribs like bows unstrung   beware the sharp end
there will be no fairytale wound

      sleep awhile, if you will
        but expect no handsome visitor

its capped heart a flask for
what?   linseed oil?
    fodder for careful creatures
      ears raised & a phosphate thump

label the provinces:

    calcaneus   carpus   cranium   femur
    ilium   mandible   maxilla   phalanges
    radius   scapula   sternum   tibia

        a rabbit atlas

Sarah K. Bell

Rain

    Rain bubble-wrapping the windows. Rain
falling as though someone ran a blade down the spines
    of fish setting those tiny backbones free. Rain
        with its squinting glance, rain

    with its rustle of descending silk. Rain, rain,
the cascading rain outrunning its own skeins in the lilting
    dark. The loquacious rain, glissading across
        the drip-garrulous leaves. Tipsy

    rain, puddling, wetting its own socks. Rain's
swirl at my feet smelling of leaf musk. Rain falling
    like seed-gobs in the street-light's tumbledown gloom.
        Sifted rain, purling, paying

    its way while its veil makes a thin distance.
Rain spiccatoing over wavelets and their hilly crests.
    Rain cashing up along the skyline of gold-minted lights.
        Rain nibbling at the grass

    with broken teeth. Crestfallen rain leaving
the road, then riffling through the lop-eared treetops.
    Rain tanglefooted, half out of its clothes. Sweeps
        of rain like hair,

    like pampas stalks, wind-tarried, bending; or tall,
ornamental, moving louchely and skew-whiff. Rain's
    drops when they begin to fly as though they're being
        shuddered off

a shaggy dog. Rain wayworn in the slippery
night, drumbling across awnings, gutters, windows, walls
   and slowing down those tittupy drops until the sky
      like a new god glozes

   with a little rollicking thunder and lets the first
light through in luteous gloops. But then more rain, more
   clouds stacking up, rain that will come down fast
      again, like grain from gunnysacks.

Judith Beveridge

In the Somme

Snow has clotted on the earth.
The body and the mind have been arrayed
for so long, the seasons folding and unfolding,
their emnity is numb.

Numb, the mind is polishing its arms; numb,
the stoic body, at its watch, shakes frost
from the hand in which it holds a scrap of bread
to a rat. The body has the empathy of flesh.

Flesh, unknown to body, is the shibboleth
by which the mind discriminates its own;
self, in body's mouth, is only *flesh* in anagram.
Mind abhors the power of the dumb.

'Dumb silence, and the awe of all millennia
spent on such reconnoissance and strife.'
The mind is at its notes again.
The body is asleep.

Judith Bishop

Outdoor Pig-keeping, 1954 & My Other Books on Farming Pigs

Pig Farming. Methods Of
was a book I wrote in 1945
tho what I knew then of
pig farming you may wonder. It is
a human enough activity.
I mean 'universal' – did they have
pigs on Easter Island, the New Guinea
highlands, did the Maori? Virgil
knew about pigs, tho I associate him, more,
with bees, my Latin education centring
on a limited number of texts –
bits of Caesar's *Gallic Wars*
or *Punic Wars* ('Carthage delenda est'?) –
& not much else. Virgil. Ideas of
pig farming might be innate. (?)
Where do correct ideas come from?
'The head, boss.' Pigs pretty much
know what they want (isn't that
often thought to be the problem,
the thing held against them?),
give it to them. 'Long pig' was somehow
special dark knowledge when I was
a schoolboy, I mean the term.
A human dish. (No one else ate it,
except the odd lion or tiger –

as a one-off: humans also
protect their own – better probably not
to eat them too often.) But, to return
to the term, 'long pig' implies knowledge
of 'pig plain' sure enough. It seemed
insulting, to me, back then – to the idea
of the human & humanity & I didn't like
to utter it. I remember once
someone telling me of an abandoned
hippy farm where they'd been producing
heroin. The pigs were fed
on scraps & excrement
& were squealing. Addicted.
Apparently the noise was horrible. I did,
at some time, sleep near where a pig
– or pigs – squealed all night. I can't remember
now whether it was simply very affecting
or whether it was specifically because it sounded
human. It was loud, incessant & frightened.
I can't remember where or when. An
abattoir. In 1945
I had not read Virgil. I do know that.
It seems we've passed this way before. In
'another life' I may have *been* a pig farmer:
I see me, late at night at a plain kitchen table
writing *Pig Farming, Methods Of.* It's
electric light – tho it could do with a stronger
bulb. I write it in a child's school exercise book.
My only daughter has died? It's hers, hardly used,
& I turn it round & start at the back? – or maybe
continue right on from where she left off.

She had been studying & had written *amo, amas,*
amat etc. The vocabulary list begins with
agricola – farmer. As I see it the farmer
does not become especially sentimental about
the exercise book. He may have done, must
have done, at some time since his daughter's death,
but now he writes. Perhaps he writes with
extra care because it is her book. Perhaps he writes
because it is her book. He has not written
anything else before. He writes now
because she is gone. She was the future
& he was content to work to see her through –
to her adult life. But now she is gone
he must make something else. He is a widower.
I was brought up by my own father,
alone, me & my sister. We kept dogs & cats
& pigeons, a horse. No pigs. Anyway,
there it is, & it has my name on it, 1945 – *Pig Farming,*
Methods Of.

Ken Bolton

After Fred Williams' *You Yangs 1*

The way spirit tracks, in brushstrokes or words, you'd have
    Buckley's
of getting it right, sensing how out here light does not fall.
    Waves of images
fill you so there's nothing but to paint, though you don't like it,
    this country
that's in you, the red dust coating everything in one place or
    the granite now,
beneath your feet an island, quartz and feldspar cooled
    beneath an ocean
millions of years departed before your arrival. The wattle an
    edged blur in distance,
melancholy of the she-oaks weird, almost human with arms
    languorous,
supine to a brutality of light that in another language might
    be what is.
Gusts gathering yellow sands, slow erosion, there is no
    foreground, no back,
harlequin mistletoe, cherry ballart, the rock before you
    holding light
sings like everything else here, a silence you seek out the
    heart of.
So you work ten canvases at once though there's no focal point,
    no cathedral
to wash time across, to track the changing planes of day, to
    assure meaning, only
what is built out of winds and dust and rock and song now half-
    heard, half-dead,
unlearnt names scattered on a map. The idea of elsewhere you
    leave behind
or end up like one of those figures in a landscape pointing the
    way ahead,

to something picturesque beyond the frame, the perspective
   warped
by some new Eden, some ancient Arcadia waiting to be
   plundered, a lie
like the emptiness gathered and named and transported here
   to build on.
Your eyes trace the scrub, manna gums and yellow gums
   scrimshawing
landscape, red gums sketch out a vertical line like a man
   practising his whole life
to say a single word, finding his bearings in a place he can only
   come to slowly.
Crossing the lava, basalt, time uncovers you, uncovers land,
   an aspect of light
so what you abstract is not self, not place, not moment but all
   these spoken
by marks, scars in a greater shared immensity, a flat
   dun-coloured space,
a stillness where the delusions of horizon have been erased,
   skins
peeled back, as if death could be cast off, its flesh left to dry in
   sun, and time
curved on itself, a husk. You watch in tongues of light, listening
   with eyes,
unearthing spirit amongst boneseed and sundew, perhaps
   love,
in daubs of skyless light, learning country, speaking it as it
   speaks you.

Michael Brennan

A Place on Earth

A young boy
is sitting by a fire
on the edge of the desert. There's a car
through the scrub behind him
pulled off to the side of the long dirt road
and a tent close by with his father in it, sleeping
already. It is late evening, nine or ten,
and he's long ago eaten: toast, baked
beans on a tin plate, burnt potatoes, tea.
1964 perhaps, or '63:
it doesn't matter what year.
He is sitting by the fire, stoked
earlier so that now it's burned back to the ancient
fire-gutted log he found and dragged here
before the sun set – burned back
so that, now the log is deep alight,
he can see a world in it: sees falling towers, forgotten
Alexandrias and Babylons,
the night markets of Wuzhou, Rangoon, Hong Kong,
sees Siegfried and the *Götterdämmerung*,
sees a huge, blood-orange sun
setting over the burnt, black
hills around him,
autos-da-fé, charred ruins, faces
staring from the flame
so beautiful they seem to scorch him,
sees the bombing and the burning of Dresden,
bodies in fiery graves, wild
midnight carnivals, sees
Moon-men and Sun-men in corroboree,

sees hearth-fires and bonfires and beakon-fires,
Etnas in their scoriac flows,
townspeople and villagers fleeing,
docks and homes and factories alight,
sees battered galleons, masts
collapsing, armadas blazing on the sea, radiant
sunrise breaking from the glowing embers
as if out of a phoenix-nest.

Something
rustles in the ti-tree, a
wallaby perhaps, night bird or
wild dog drawn by the fire,
and he looks up from his dreaming, sees the huge
darkness of the night and the vast
canopy of unknown, unnameable stars,
a night so infinite, this night,
it will never leave him.
Time and again he will look up
– for sixty or for seventy years, luck holding – and it
will always be there: before him
the fire, behind him
his father sleeping, that something
rustling in the undergrowth,
and about him the galaxies turning, the still
point of his being,
a place on earth,
gift beyond measure.

David Brooks

Ninox strenua

Ninox strenua, the Powerful Owl, stands
sixty centimetres tall and has a wingspan
of almost one hundred and fifty, 'defends'
a territory of up to fifteen hundred hectares
though hunts much more widely, has a beak
tough as a bolt-cutter, mates for life, lives
on a diet of ring-tailed possum and sweet
sugar glider, is endangered and rarely seen
though its two-note call is familiar
to anyone who listens to the bush at night.
In our catchment there's at least one breeding pair,
working its way as the months pass
anti-clockwise over an area fifteen by
fifteen kilometres – two hundred
and twenty-five square.
The local Wildlife Rescue Service
will not release young possums into the scrub
at any time near the full moon and until
they've checked the raptors' whereabouts.
Ninox strenua is rumoured to kill
up to thirty ring-tailed possums per night, and, almost
human in its wastefulness,
eats only the brain.

David Brooks

breath

I come from the dead zone with clap trap jaw and clankin gait
and bulletswhistle is my song
halloooo coooweeeeee goes burnin down
    thegreengullylacedwithferns
curlin coyly hideaway and low-dippin currawong calls

my locomotive breath announces me, my breath in the darlin
    morn
and my heart jumpin with the joy of jump-up to that
carnivorous constabulary dead-set keen to eat us all alive

damn if I'll not slip from the steam of their winter broth and
    when they aim
– and only then – then in my wrath I'll rain damnation down
upon their tick-pocked heads

callin all you lustrous coots and laddies hidden in the
    bloody bracken come
or lead-riddled, swimmin out the ether, bound for
    heaven or hell which entertainment
we can wait indefinitely for to see
for all scabby-knee kids never given a brumby's
    chance
astride my last I'm a moveable fort
a hero with breath forged in a fearful fire
June's bite an ice of iron

stop your coughin don't dream I will leave you

wrote I needed no lead or powder
wrote words would be louder

I lied

Jen Jewel Brown

Blue Glow

crows crark
over darlinghurst,
we order
black beer

*

sitting on wet sand
watching steepling surf,
a huge dirtywater tide
threatens bondi

*

your sudden
and beautiful exit
frightened me

*

I was going to say
how we took cocaine
and danced, in ultimo,
when we were older
than we should have been

but it was your funeral,
it was too sorrowful,
now I'm stuck
with platitudes
you'd find funny,
anyway
I can say anything
in a poem
you'll never read

    *

artificially overlit
groves of myrtle
staged for you,
and never televised
(not as if we didn't try)

the secrets
you mentioned
on your second last day
are secret still

    *

three storms in three hours,
hailstones ripping holes
in the nasturtium leaves.
blackout –
using a torch to find a candle

    *

I'd never tell anyone,
but just look at this,
what I'm doing now

daily crumplings

will this
take my mind off things
when
I could simply spend
more and more time
watching tv?

      *

to be here
knowing you're not
gets me down

the latest person
I had to tell
said
'she was someone
I always thought
I would see again'

      *

you're not around,
you're only a dream,
always
so anti-sentimental
you drank whisky
after everyone else
gave it up

  *

you loved
the halloween parade song
and the wooster group

our own theatre
was courageous,
not 'showy',
and failed
its experiment

new york
can wait –
I'm sorry, new york,
you'll have to wait

  *

helplessly,
I placed two perfect
nasturtium leaves
in the card from morocco
and brought them
to your delirium

  *

you read my prose
from over twenty years ago
at your mother's funeral

the piece that says
'we don't die alone'
and that
'maybe love
comes to us from the dead'

I decided
not to read it
for you

two decades later
I'm not at all
certain of it

    *

I'd like to sleep
tonight
all night long
in the blue glow

(in memoriam Jan McKemmish)

Pam Brown

harbinger

1.
siliconed stacks of glass
reflect the harbour
miracle of gliding windows
multiplying the view an
extended prologue
to an opaque parable

this is my postcard city
my teatowel my snowdome
my archival ferry ticket, my
effusive chalice point of
view point my malaise
yes my swamp of leisure –
how a cruise ship, 'liner'
tracy says, slides through
your waters like a
trojan horse

2.
why was a japanese light plane
able to complete its reconnaissance
mission flying in and out of sydney
harbour right up to the bridge and
not be intercepted, in 1942; urban
legend where is your tee-shirt

3.
this is where flying boats
departed and arrived to
and from 'the islands', the rose
bay flying boat base, hear
them purr across easy fronds
of post war summer waters,
frangipani suitcases of new
pacific dreams; i'm happy
sucking jaffas on the slap up
steps of the nearby rsl; jason
and the argonauts were never
moored near my palm tree

4.
sit on the seat outside
elizabeth bay house imagine
the historic gardens of alexander
and elizabeth mcleay rolling
down towards the harbour 'a sylvan
coup d'oeil' said the sydney gazette,
'a little paradise' nodded dr. george
bennett; 'a few english showers would
improve it' wrote georgiana lowe

my eyes reach over to the bay
around to darling point and
the hills above the heads, and so
continues lowe 'the bays are
innumerable, and resemble the scotch
salt-water lochs'; this area of sydney
around what is now nicknamed betty
bay was once known as blacktown,
macquarie having had it reserved [that
is 'put aside'] for the aborigines

5.
just hours before he died
i took his pocket radio and
earphones, that he would use at
the cricket, to the sea wall at rose bay
and sat on the ledge behind the shops,
just along from the demolished
wintergarden theatre where we'd seen
so many movies, stories rising from
the harbour on a velvet screen; and
i noted a small ferry crossing
the entrance to the bay; 'mad about
you' was playing loudly in my head, a
gust of windsurfers moving suddenly
into view

joanne burns

London Fields

The night my girl flew to Paris
the phone rang and I thought
it's her but heard the voice
of a man I did not know saying
I had fucked up and he knew where
I was and was coming to get me.
His voice had a Kray Twins sort
of truth and sneered as I said
I don't know you I've never met you.
I'm coming to get you he said
I'm coming there to get you now.

That we lived in a flat atop
a large Edwardian home and thus
I had two front doors between me
and that voice was of some comfort,
though not complete. Some days later
when our old blue Triumph Herald
was stolen the police found it
a few streets away the wiper blades
twisted oddly like the arms of a man
imprisoned in a dungeon somewhere
down the East End or so it felt.

I got casual work in Fleet Street
left the Reuters building at dusk
got off at Highgate. By the tube
was a pub The Woodman where I drank
a pint or so then walked the dark
Queen's Wood ten minutes to my door
love poems in my head for my girl
as I strolled beneath the trees.
One night voices hard and close
I heard two men crashing through
the woods walking fast with purpose.

Years later home in Australia I read
of Dennis Nilsen a former army cook
he had killed fifteen boys and men
picked them up in The Woodman
drugged killed and butchered
buried parts flushed others fed
entrails to animals got found out
only after neighbours complained
of blocked and smelly drains
in his flat in Cranley Gardens
at the end of our street.

Larry Buttrose

After the Headlines

A city's candy lights are seen through cataracts.
At dusk, the quay shimmers, conceals its mystery.
Juanita, the dead model, suicides off The Gap
seem nothing in comparison to the ferry's claim.
After the news, I dreamt about the pleasure boat,
water gushing starboard, the sudden amputation,
a figure skater's dress ballooning as she drowned
with a last pirouette to perfect her disappearance.
It wasn't a spectacle, or a Greek tragedy, but sad
to think of her body decomposing, a fine residue
of minerals for plankton and algae, for curious fish.
Days before there was a plane crash in Jogjakarta.
Award-winning journalists were burnt alive like fuel
for media barons and technophiles. It's strange
how we crave the visual, buying and selling images
of tsunamis, flash flooding, avian flu epidemics.
I heard patients in the waiting room speak about
this latest disaster, as if fate's occasion signalled
some compelling universal law that I should dread.
Sitting at my desk, I scanned the day's reports,
checking blood counts, electrolytes, cardiographs.
Whatever I've learnt in medicine, something slips
from the palanquin, refusing death, revived by more
than IV adrenaline, narcaine, or shock can provide.
Like screen addicts we rehash the myths. The ultimate
getaway is a dream Corvette for our reticent ghosts.

Michelle Cahill

Ithaka

Laistrygonians and Cyclops,
angry Poseidon – do not fear them. — CAVAFY, 'Ithaka'

Cavafy, lying alone in his own bed
for five years, ten years, dreaming of bright boys,
said, enjoy yourselves! And anything you fear, you
have brought with you, on this journey to Ithaka ...

Lying alone unsleeping in this good house
that is not mine, the bright day gone to teeming night,
the thought-bark ground ashore again
on this old Ithaka, a slaughter of servants and suitors –

is this Cyclops? the single eye of night that is too dark to close,
the skylight squadroning love into wicked shapes, the murderer
stowed away above me in the loft? my eye
that seeing nothing, sees all this? I lie awake and wait

for the batter at the door – sit up each time and look
as headlights crunch through trees, three in two hours,
then away. But he too must have *known*: as I *know*, lying
there, truth homing on us like a psychopath – the mind jags

its needle, skips and skips – our poems all
nostalgia; too old, finished, no one now will ever love us.
I turn on the light, take a pill – the metal cup reflects
my look – for what is Ithaka but this

knowledge of my own soul?
Sleep the safe journey, Ithaka arrival, waking.
An old, a respectable trick, I've done it, this making
a perfectly ended poem that tells the reader 'don't

waste your time on endings': art as round and finished
as the lives of the dead, to celebrate the virtue
of life's unfinish. The incomplete reader
staring in from outside polished glass, trying to enjoy

her ceaseless churning – *that* is the poem, that *is* the poem,
that is me, this is really living ... 'and if you find her poor ...'
if fear is your waiting wife, you'll count all night
the Alexandrias burned, isles bounded, stars fixed, and rise

to a self as settled as a curse: home
of every terrible return, whole and unchanged, still
knowing the meaning of these Ithakas.

Elizabeth Campbell

Intervention Pay Back

I love my wife   she right skin for me   pretty one my wife
young one   found her at the next community over   across
the hills   little bit long way   not far

and from there she give me good kids   funny kids mine   we
always laughing   all together   and that wife   she real
good mother   make our wali real nice   flowers and grass
patch and chickens   I like staying home with my kids

and from there I build cubby house   yard for the horse   see
I make them things from left overs   from the dump   all the
leftovers from fixing the houses   and all the leftovers I build
cubby house and chicken house

and in the house we teach the kids   don't make mess   go
to school learn good so you can work round here later   good
job   good life   and the government will leave you alone

and from there tjamu and nana tell them the story   when
the government was worse   rations   government make up
all the rules   but don't know culture   can't sit in the sand
oh tjamu and nana   they got the best story   we always
laughing us mob

and from there night time when we all asleep   all together
on the grass patch   dog and cat and kids   my wife and
me   them kids they ask really good questions about the olden
days   about today   them real ninti them kids   they gunna
be right

and from there come intervention   John Howard   he make new rules   he never even come to see us   how good we was doing already   Mal Brough   he come with the army   we got real frightened true   thought he was gonna take the kids away   just like tjamu and nana bin tell us

I run my kids in the sand hills   took my rifle up there and sat   but they was all just lying   changing their words all the time   wanting meeting today and meeting tomorrow   we was getting sick of looking at them   so everyone put their eyes down   and some even shut their ears

and from there I didn't care too much   just kept working fixing the housing   being happy working hard   kids go to school   wife working hard too   didn't care too much   we was right   we always laughing us mob   all together

but then my wife she come home crying   says the money in quarantine but I didn't know why they do that   we was happy   not drinking and fighting   why they do that we ask the council   *to stop the drinking and protect the children*   hey you know me ya bloody mongrel I don't drink   and I look after my kids   I bloody fight ya you say that again   *hey settle down we not saying that   Mal Brough saying that   don't you watch the television   he making the rules for all the mobs   every place Northern Territory   he real cheeky whitefella   but he's the boss we gotta do it*

and from there I tell my wife she gets paid half   half in hand half in the store   her money in the store now   half and half me too   all us building mob   but I can't buy tobacco   or work boots   you only get the meat and bread   just like the mission days   just like tjamu and nana tell us

{38}

and from there I went to the store to get meat for our supper
but the store run out   only tin food left   so I asked for some
bullets I'll go shoot my own meat   but sorry they said   you
gotta buy food   that night I slept hungry   and I slept by
myself   thinking about it

and from there the government told us our job was finish
the government bin give us the sack   we couldn't believe it
we been working CDEP for years   slow way we park the truck
at the shed   just waiting for something   for someone with
tobacco

the other men's reckon   fuck this   drive to town for the
grog   but I stayed with my kids   started watching the
television   trying to laugh   not to worry   just to be like
yesterday

and from there the politician man says *I give you real job*   tells
me to work again   but different   only half time sixteen
hours   but I couldn't understand   it was the same job
as before   but more little   less pay   and my kids can't
understand   when they come home from school   why I
can't buy the lolly for them like I used to before   I didn't
want to tell them   I get less money for us now

and from there they say my wife earns too much money   I
gonna miss out again   I'm getting sick of it   don't worry
she says   I'll look after you   but I know that's not right way
I'm getting shame   my brother   he shame too   he goes to
town drinking   leaves his wife behind   leaves his kids

and from there I drive round to see tjamu   he says his money
in the store too   poor bloke   he can't even walk that far
and I don't smile   I look at the old man   he lost his smile
too   but nana she cook the damper and roo tail   she trying
to smile   she always like that

and from there when I get home   my wife gone to town with
the sister in law   she gone look for my brother   he might
be stupid on the grog   he not used to it   she gotta find him
might catch him with another woman   make him bleed
drag him home

and from there my wife   she come back   real quiet   tells
me she went to casino   them others took her   taught her
the machines   she lost all the money   she lost her laughing

and from there all the kids bin watching us   quiet way   not
laughing around   so we all go swimming down the creek
all the families there together   we happy again   them boys
we take them shooting   chasing the malu in the car   we
real careful with the gun   not gonna hurt my kids no way

and from there my wife   she sorry   she back working hard
save the money   kids gonna get new clothes   I gonna get
my tobacco and them bullets   but she gone change again
getting her pay   forgetting her family   forget yesterday
only thinking for town   with the sister in law

and my wife   she got real smart now   drive for miles all
dressed up   going to the casino with them other kungkas
for the Wednesday night draw

I ready told you I love my kids   I only got five   two pass away already   and I not complaining bout looking after my kids   no way   but when my wife gets home   if she spent all the money   not gonna share with me and the kids

I might hit her   first time

Ali Cobby Eckermann

---

wali – house, tjamu – grandfather, ninti – clever, malu – kangaroo, kungkas – women

North Durras Caravan Park

1.
Coastal:

yesterday the clearest beach / today north of Durras
south Durras sailing away / flooding

with wet gum forest misty mountain hop
sucking up glass channels like canticles like livid

creeks manic veins wriggling on the inlet where
is Durras / if not north

south is it sailing out with the salty fresh
water of a conscience? It was further back down

there / two figures threading (they came
together ...) threading together the sand

and the sky their intimate geographies a single map.

2.
In the distance the retired wives club chatters
in Technicolor wings singing

orchestras by the tennis court flash
your bouncing body on a pasture lay

out shells / like wet black words
on a white page I'm thinking

in terms of tennis / smacking one ball
back but always the ball it's coming towards you reaching

past   in terms of threads
between in and out, empiricism

and heart.

3.
If you were on a balcony above Durras in the teen-teen-
teen oftheorthe bribble-gribble ofthe

of the wheezing-whine of the young magpie your
mum hopping about stabbing scraps your music

screaming *Content is a slippery glimpse*
if you had the world at hand the body fresh

your entrance to the ocean wrapped around you
southern capillaries pumping through wind flesh

and questions of papery bark peeling
as she opens her wings like pages to be written

in North Durras …
the longer route crumbles like a sandy bank.

4.
Doubting that there's the kind hand of late spring
gentle waves squashed up matter regurgitated – even

the magpie's dirty grey feathers and the other dream / mine
of pretence to unorigin of a gaseous nomad but

of the two – the bird and the dream – that magpie
crystallising / flying through worlds to sing lines

always searching for the open into which any black
and white soul can continue

singing the line the thin-/sun line
I'd snort I'm that sure

of the excitement in a pulse: now / being now
time. Rising. Because

the *lovely stuff, you know,*
is livelier.

Stuart Cooke

From the following poems by Peter Minter:
'sucking up glass channels' ('Lust'),
'Content is a slippery glimpse' ('Linguige'),
'lovely stuff, you know, is *livelier*' ('Odalisk').

Expeditions with W.G. Sebald

You think you want congruence,
our imaginations closer
than the rings of Saturn,
yours just enclosed in mine.—SUSAN LUDVIGSON

I. WALKING

Let's list as you loved to:
Jerusalemstraat, Nachtegaalstraat,
Pelikanstraat, Paradijsstraat,
Immerseelstraat –
street names accumulate and empty as the long begats
of the Bible, as the smudged faces in photographs,
whose uneager looks, whose knowing looks,
are husks of insects piled up as if
one name on top of another,
one corpse concealing another,
can be said.

Let's walk again
in Suffolk, as you did:
see those same compressed horizons of land,
the calm Deben, the laden,
low skies, pools of ashes
at Auschwitz.

Words are words.
Our shovels, our nails.

Can I tell your tale
of how, lost on a walk near Benacre Broad,
you came upon a brackish lake?
Always for me, that word leaps out like
a struggling fish – *brackish!*
Meticulous writer, did you
bend over the water,
take some of the lake
into your mouth?

Or can I tell you of my dream
in which, discovering
some power of the hands
I turned a bare woods to blossom
and then, at a whim,
sent each white
flower
snowflaking to the ground?

Are there not two possible gods
also walking the world:
one who raises His arms
and changes the very nature of things –
and another, hunchbacked with effort,
who bends to taste, eternally,
that which He already knows
is bitter?

II. Fishing

'Dying,'
said Ingmar Bergman,
'is a very wise arrangement.'

Perhaps. For years, fishing with my grandfather,
I made him take from my hook
the herring, skipjack, flathead, black bream,
so that, once, on an expedition with a friend,
neither of us knew how to make the kill.
I was sure you broke the neck
at the gills, but she, inspired,
took the knife and sawed off its head.

Such things stay,
as if, inexplicably, we trawled,
and caught all sorts of things in our nets.
I didn't think of it when, in the Louvre,
I came upon Fra Angelico's *Le martyre
des saints Cosme et Damien*
though perhaps I should have;
those saints on their knees, the violence
of their beheading, and their halos,
lingering even over the decapitated heads,
as light is inclined to,
on what we have severed.

'Perhaps it is no coincidence,'
you said, 'that to dream of fish
is said to mean death.'
And, how much we have mourned,
or how little,
day in, day in.

The men of Sicily fish for tunny
as they have for thousands of years.
Hauled, stunned and bleeding,
from the sea – one of the fishermen
will always place his brown hands
over the tunny's great eyes,
in order to ease its panic.

Shevaun Cooley

Maldon, 991 A.D.

after the Anglo-Saxon

The heart sank under such grey skies:
no good way to spin 4,000 Vikings
waiting restless in their longboats
for the tide to bring them closer,
one stroke closer, one horn-blast away,
to my end. (For it was all about me.)
Then Byrhtnoth began to array us,
the forlorn, the foredoomed, the feymen.
He paced and gave counsel, edgy, asteed,
on how we might stand tight
this happy ground. He bade us hold
our roundshields rightly fast.
I hardly listened. O distant clouds.
Dismounting, he went to his hearth-band;
what is it with this gangly grace
before death? I felt an outsider
to laughter. Out there the Vikings sang,
that was more like it, something eerie
to get spooked about, distracted by;
and the world so tenderly
unveiling its final unveiling.

Luke Davies

A Dry Winter
Some Observations About Rain

1.
In the night, the birds hold their breath,
stillness descends in a low cloud.

The ear dilates, every attentive leaf
awaits the arrival of this rain –

an elemental transition from dry to damp.
Listen, you can hardly hear its outward breath

on the tin roof. In the morning,
grass and earth are wet and everything

but the mercuric globe in the nasturtium leaf
is translucent.

2.
These drops thud like water bombs on the warm concrete.
Individualists, each outdoes the next in size, velocity.

They fall to earth perpendicular from a great height,
spurred on by canons of thunder.

3.
The easterly is an eraser, rubbing out first horizon,
then hard grey ocean, then the silhouette of gum trees

at distant water's edge. A swift operator, it obliterates paddocks
and middle distance then hits in a squall like bullet fire.

Glass and trees strain not to crack and snap. Indoors is
    chromatic,
the rest is black and white. This rain moves on swiftly

leaving sun and silence in its wake, the house creaking
along its trusses from time to time, like a ship after a storm
    at sea.

4.
This rain is augured by an alteration of light: premature dusk,
a fluorescence in the air that outlines gutter, tree and leaf

against a back-lit, photographer's-screen sky. Telegraph wires
are prominent. In parks and gardens chlorophyll permeates
    the air;

red makes its presence brilliantly felt in flowering gum, fuchsia.
This rain arrives at a forty-five degree angle from the north.

At autumn's end its sound on the tin roof is a continuum of
    rice grain.
It leaves on a suspended cadence, the air electric with
    imminence.

5.
Mostly, too little rain falls here.
There is only the silence of the sun.

Even in winter after low skies
and the impression of damp

for days and weeks, the earth is dry as dust
under trees. Cracks refuse to close up

in the cold months. This makes rain exotic.
Something to pay attention to.

Sarah Day

The Ties My Sister Makes

The silk ties my sister makes
lie sheathed in plastic sheets
in their pigeon holes
in the factory
beneath the volcano.
They hold all the colours of the sea
and are scaled like fishes too
so that when I first see them
laid out in their obedient ranks
I want to exclaim like Willmouse to Shelley
at the Roman fish market
che belle cose!
My sister's ties
will be dispatched about the world,
their underwater silvers and greens
flashing in the dark aquariums of shop windows.
I think of all the necks they will encircle,
the men who will make their deft adjustments
and the women who will stroke them and roll them away
with socks or hang them inside wardrobe doors,
unaware of my sister's clever hands
and of her name
inside the label
beating out its syllables
silently next to their husband's hearts.
And I think, too, of my sister's voice
in the sunlit factory
beneath the volcano
saying *Please, please
take for your friends.*

Lucy Dougan

Letter to John Forbes

lit up in a window
with a burger & glass
of African *chenin blanc*

I'm reading the later Creeley
on Charing Cross Road

you, ten years back
in limbo (Melbourne)
of which you made the best

I inhabit an England
you mightn't recognise
though you would have read
the fine print that led here

(the market *didn't* decide
in your case).

will I echo Le Douanier, who
celebrated Picasso as 'traditional',
himself as 'modern'?

maybe

this notebook's
no 'art pad',
nor is this place

(everyone behind the counter
is from Poland)

the music:
'I am a cauliflower'
misheard from the Stone Roses

opposite: BUDWEISER,
ENGLISH BREAKFAST
'OPEN',

the only art here
is civic (a 'water feature'
from the seventies)

the buses all head north
to Clapton Pond,
but I'm southbound
for The Cut, Southwark,

poetry, spotlit
on a tiny stage

Laurie Duggan

The Maze

Mud is what she remembers most,
the kind that sucks and slurps

as it betrays the body,
quicksand pulling her to where

air is thick with gravel,
where her body is a battlefield.

The lump they lifted clear
was stone to her, its hurtful

drumming like a dance of anger
vanished in the thick seams

that now bind her breast back to itself.
She is lost, underground, without

Orpheus or any guide. This is the maze
without the minotaur; where the fresh

blue cut of sky is a fading memory.
Mostly she knows this is a fairy tale,

a grim one, where swathes of hair
are hacked off to plait a rope

to lead her to the surface, or else to lay
in patterns in the darkening woods

to puzzle her way back. There is no one
else at all, just this body

and her once brave head spinning
under the soil's glittering stars.

This is the journey where a woman
is shape-changed to a youth whose virtue

defeats evil, craving courage
instead of head-in-hands howling,

finding kindness where normally she would not look.
It is the looking that is most difficult,

facing the future with a clear-eyed gaze that claims:
send black ravens, dragons from the west country,

send hags, crones, mad men, wild horses;
I will find my way home.

Adrienne Eberhard

Murray Dreaming

It's not the sharks
Sliding mere inches from his upturned face
Through warps of water where the tunnel arcs
Transparent overhead,
Their lipless jaws clamped shut, extruding teeth,
Their eyes that stare at nothing, like the dead,
Staring at him; it's not the eerie grace
Of rays he stood beneath,
Gaping at their entranced slow-motion chase

That is unending;
It's not the ultra-auditory hum
Of ET cuttlefish superintending
The iridescent craft
Of their lit selves, as messages were sent,
Turning the sight of him they photographed
To code: it is not this that left him dumb
With schoolboy wonderment
Those hours he wandered the aquarium.

It is that room,
That room of Murray River they had walled
In glass and, deep within the shifting gloom
And subtle drifts of sky
That filtered down, it seemed, from the real day
Of trees and bird light many fathoms high,
The giant Murray cod that was installed
In stillness to delay
All that would pass. The boy stood there enthralled.

Out in the day
Again, he saw the famous streets expound
Their theories about speed, the cars obey,
Racing to catch the sun,
The loud fast-forward crowds, and thought it odd
That in the multitudes not everyone
Should understand as he did the profound
Profession of the cod,
That held time, motionless, unknown to sound.

In bed at night,
Are his eyes open or is this a dream?
The room is all dark water, ghosted light,
And midway to the ceiling
The great fish with its working fins and gills
Suspended, while before it glide the reeling
And see-through scenes of day, faintly agleam,
Until their passage stills
And merges with the deep unmoving stream.

Stephen Edgar

The Big Splash

A mannequin parade watches
every other eye
where the oar blades leave blazing
trails of phosphorescence
When I turned up
the party in question
had a Botticelli
innocence owned a small
but brilliant shop
full of forget-me-nots
& odd clocks Now
frocks & sandals are
for that matter necessary
rowing across for days
I hoot at the moon if I must
perhaps not Pay the ferryman
something A penny for your
thoughts These crash
dummies are unsalable he
said Unusually he pictured
his addenda as pudenda
i.e. *loc. cit.* etc. which was
admiral & inseparable
from this season's big
splash upended & totally
overboard & so embarked
for nowhere long forgotten
but not gone

Chris Edwards

Between

In the thin place between the word and the thing,
at the wall's inside, old wires intertwine
and cockroaches are the hieroglyphs of home.

I take your hand in these last nights and wait
beside the Styx on a green bank that runs to the wood,
in the thin place between the word and the thing.

And we stand all night gazing at the hard water
and cannot see the other side. Still in the ward
the neon obscures the hieroglyphs of home.

We've come this far but are stubborn at the pier
beside the boat's bob and the oars unused
in the thin place between the word and the thing.

And our breaths intertwine on the world's edge
– I've stood inside the Newgrange tomb – like
three coils that are the hieroglyphs of home.

A speck on the near horizon! Charon comes
but not tonight. And my fingers tell you I can't go
past the thin place between the word and the thing,
nor write the way for you, in the hieroglyphs of home.

Anne Elvey

From *The Correspondence*

LETTER IV: ON REALITY

We crossed the seaward field
with the air heavy against us,
our heels mining canticles from clay.
Look, you said, this is real.
The boats decay on their painters
and no one lives to sail them.
Later I saw a woman walking
past us with a lamp, illuminating

nothing but the stones
that lay broken under our feet.
I wanted suddenly to understand
the world's darker evidence,
as though the raw wager of death
skilled our souls for a greater yield.

LETTER VI: ON MOVEMENT

And so I commit myself
to the first arrivals of spring,
bold as the icicles that break
ahead of me. The hills are a magnet
for solar sequences. There is the rock
where we slept during winter,
crowned by a small skull –
I am glad to see it.

Our words are slow
despite all this motion,
the cold soil in reluctant thaw.
What more is there to say?
The sky strings up worn pennons
of fulfilment and frustration.

LETTER VII

A faulted sweetness
thrown to the world's edge –
that is desire.
     I want you
to see things as I do. Your body
dissolves and is remade. Mine is bound
to follow.
    My eyes
find you everywhere, a cracked plate,
an isolated tree, the ghostly visage
in a car window.

Four limbs
balanced in the centre,
a devoted subject of grief.
       The scene fades.
Carry my obsession past me
to the quick of feeling.

Kate Fagan

Surfers Paradise (Qld)/ Reporting for the Night Watch

Across the very busy road,
Surf rips cause many deaths.

Along the sheltered waterways,
Inside the glamour hotels,

The vowels are distorted,
Consonants dumbed down

In bondage, and in servitude,
Work and sleep, work and sleep,

A perpetual mutual accolade,
Well, the enemy could be within.

Weather-beaten vehicles cruise past,
Loud music, surfboards attached ...

Can you see beyond the flagpoles,
Can you see beyond the buoys?

Whoever gets there first, wins,
A tenuous, high-rise spectacle,

Mirrored from here to eternity,
In the Lobbies, multiple Lifts.

Outside, on the manicured lawns,
The guarded walkways, driveways,

The future is fixed, as in cement.
'Calling from the trees, Intruder!'

In the deserted gardens,
With tropical trees, huge,

And of fragrant loveliness,
A bird may still come closer,

Will look at you sideways,

'Reporting for the night watch'

Jeltje Fanoy

muzak to view the city with

Muzak makes its originals grungy makes
everything real tough.
If i hold my pseudo baby tight i participate
in muzak & remember when

My love, has so much in him he tastes
Like a cloud, im sorry,
For going so far,

Being reckless in making friends

i hope night calms the polar bear

we miss the transition, go beyond The stripped
lyric into nothing. The banal resurfaces
well phew, its effects, cause feelings strong enough
a harsh motto from sugar apter, or erykah badu

this isnt beginning a sentence
empty street man with pink umbrella.

Prepared

Michael Farrell

Notes on Art and Dying
19.10.2008 ... *How to paint a rose*

A glass case displays the steps for painting a rose. It is like looking down through still water at a catalogue of the artist's mind. First, the watercolours on white paper: orange-red, orange-purple, purple-red ... like a row of summer icy-poles melting. Second: words in neat rows of type on the page: *'the rose grows in the walled gardens of Highgrove and is the most glowing of reds oranges and purples – at times I had to blink to rest my eyes from its brilliance.'* The finished botanical lies beside the words. A single red rose, head composed high on its stem, elegant, vigorous, more luminous than its foil of white. Like the first and final drafts of a poem. The completed rose is perfect in every real detail: emblematic, cultivated to sharp points of lineage, the petals soft as blood. The real rose lies beside its representation. How do you draw a rose dying?

Susan Fealy

Inspired by Anne O'Connor's botanical paintings, Mornington Peninsula Regional Gallery.

Mother Looking into Her Son's Bedroom

His body lodges in edges
of his mother's front room.
Comics sprawl the floor.
Cat's piss smirches the air.

In his mind, earth has stiffened.
Heels clamp, teeth chip and
crumble. Most days, eyes
swish like salt in a pan,
then shut. To look, stings.

Decades of friendship, he
remains bedridden. Once,
with a surfer's frame, he'd ribbon
through Bronte's tides. Every
Saturday, with mates, fry
eggs on hot, waxed boards.

Next week, the legal aid
at 2 p.m. The past begins
again: police rants,
Kentucky Fried Chicken,
threats to die if the pension
ends. Running out of cares.

Johanna Featherstone

The Boot Left in the Snow

He had a salamander's excess of wet skin.
Brooding in enigmatic tattoos, his body flashing
like an excited toxic octopus. My song slewed
in his ear. He didn't understand that this channel
is always full of the disappointed bones
of wishful thinkers. A seal smothered in rust
coloured snow sniffs at a woman's sealskin boots
and fur-lined toes. On wild arctic plains under borealis
light, feet trip on a raised crack and ooze with yellow.
Bowheads sing beneath sheets of icy shadows
late into nights of summer's equinox. My song pierces him
with calls of pale birds nesting in distant rookeries. Hunger
taunts the sled dogs scoffing meagre rations of dinner
before slumping into exhausted shivers of skin. I play
his own trick back to him, lifting my voice an octave
to seduce the ears of his animals. He will learn the hardship
of spring where bear meets bear and caribou meets caribou.
The song I sing is full of grass and ice
grinding between the molars of a herd of musk oxen.
He loses his mind in the low drone of frozen water
straining across the crack and crash of cliffs.

Near islands dense with seal pups suckling milk
a young humpback spy-hops at the prow of a Norwegian
whale hunter's ship. A jet ski 50 km away, strains in a painful
pitch to shift its burden of carcasses. Three men leave a bar
with loaded shotguns. A baby fur seal's random cry
makes a brief comeback in the wilderness. Shells full of pearls
snap shut against breakers and decibel-loaded chargers drown
the grace of starfish walking softly over coral. In his rough palms
jackfish thump and red-footed penguins twitch upside down
before being impaled on a hook. The man bound to his mast
sobs in the presence of deep fractures. His ship's oak ribs crack
and groan between crushing floes of ice congealing around
his hull. The bear with no name who knows itself as bear,
remembers the man who taught his thigh its painful limp.
A seal of no fixed shape watches. An albatross abandons
its rare eggs to catch an unseasonable current of weather.

Jayne Fenton Keane

Exile

there is no story
just letters in the sky
the cormorants form
when
flying
in changing formations
their feathers are not waterproof
you bought him an umbrella
although these birds are well adapted
to life in and around
water
he wasn't dressed for Melbourne weather

like eggs
hope and belief are self-contained

the peaceful dove
builds
a flimsy nest
so that the future is vulnerable to predators

the brown warbler's song
goes up in scale like a question
keeping
finality at bay

the yellow-throated honey-eater
takes wool
from clothing and floor rugs
it is not distressed
by snow
rain
death is an umbrella that doesn't keep off the rain

tears came to his eyes
when you leant
across
the café table
took a thread from his top
for its nest lining
goldfinches have been seen taking
cobwebs from clotheslines

the nest is neat
cup shaped
made of grasses, cobwebs, strong fibres,
with a lining of down or soft material

this bird witnessed
the crucifixion
it tried to pull the thorns
from the crown
was left
with blood
on its
face
this is why
these birds
are so often
found
near
thorn bushes
this is why
when you asked
him
if he was
attached to
the bar stool

three hours later you
saw
him
in a romantic embrace
with the stool
on the dance
floor
he is like Christ
in that he has *lived hard and will die young*

the egrets
walk with wings drooping
hunched
as if they are sick
waiting for the nest blow
eyes
downcast
James Dean scuffing feet

full of their own self-importance
the Indian Myna's nest is crude and
untidy, made of grass and often the
paper of torn poems

the palm-cockatoo blushes
the red patches on its cheeks
turn redder when …
what happens when we *lose the story*
we mimic ourselves like drongos
'I'm not a single-mother, never seen a double mother'

it moves you like a sun dial
relaxing in the downpour

his flattery and promises
only
making you realise
the depths
of your aloneness

there is a story
of a small boy
who ran
around
and around
a perched owl
convinced
that the bird's head
was following
him
in unbroken
revolutions
when really his
reverse head turns
between acceptance and enemy
rejection and friend
lover or self
partner and other
were too quick for you to observe them

Claire Gaskin

Sound Piece

Geometric rows of drawers in the curiosity cabinet,
and hidden compartments that open onto imprecise
chronometry: in the top left, gardens of giant kelp

seething and gurgling against mottled orange rocks;
traces of seaweed and decomposition. The next drawer
slides open to the sound of rain without it, and the plinking

of flags blowing against flagpoles. Too hazardous,
holding the specimens still enough to pin firmly through
their torsos. A weathered tray replays the rhythmic note

of a baby sister sucking her dummy in the night,
heard as measured adult steps in the bushy darkness
beyond the sliding glass door. Another drawer holds

the slicing of a green apple into wafers with the worn
brown knife. In a middle compartment: the swish
of a letter dropped into the post box; an unaccompanied

motet, forty voices wide, rising into dense layers
of amplitude to fill the many-spaced time-piece,
its fallible classification. A lower drawer consists

of walking into the threads of old spider webs, and
the distant grumble of a bus arriving at last. This section
for sea creatures: the skeleton of a small fish, fossilised

with eerie blank eyes and slender barbel; the graduated
spiral of a shell so perfect it doesn't seem real, then
a stripe of sunlight across our shins, leading

to a shelf that preserves the pang of a muted light
gleaming from the windows of your last house.

Jane Gibian

A Description of the Storm Glass and Guide to Its Use in Forecasting Weather

1.
A sealed dome of glass where crystals,
by an alchemy 'more precise than precision', unmake
and make still grottoes that recede
from its blue-doubled curves as if epitomes
of fantastical ambition –

A replica, it would embarrass
by the overconfidence of intention, except those crystals
in colours of obduracy, which is to say,
uncoloured, blank of eye, formalise the inwardness
of weather and contract

hemispheres of wind to a decorative instance:
a northerly forms in it 'leaves of fern or yew' and, by that
    version of tact
which gives volume to silence,
its crystals retreat from tempest into the vanishing point
of their dimension –

2.
In a Storm Glass crystals
with the exactness peculiar to foreboding make neural
flare shapes: ultrasound-
coloured threads cross-stitched with blank, as of sensation
excised and here, preserved in light.

It is tomorrow's weather
haunting a small room. Clouds, which hurry for no one,
which, amassing, betoken
that undifferentiated grudge some call ambition, here confide
motive without gesture

As if to say There is
another world. It is in this one, this sealed glass, structure
of feeling in place of thought
where images fold into images the way a child disappears
into the film in which she plays herself –

3.
Original of Snow Domes –
soundproof rooms of repeating weather, of figurines in
time-lapse flurries
of glitter rain – a Storm Glass, shaken, begins again its
self-assembling: workmanship

of an almost substanceless
precision. It is reinventing weather as a daydream. Only its
double-curved glass,
which builds in parallax, makes it more like an instrument
of hauntings, as if to say

He gave his whole life
to become his idea of himself. So, tireless and without
the extravagance of waves,
a Storm Glass amasses its precarious adornment, this needlework
in quartz, mistakable for regret –

Lisa Gorton

Classifying the Animals

There are those that in the distance seem a swarm of gnats
those that with their barking try to rally us in a campaign
    against the stars
those that torment their prey
those that follow both sides of an argument
those that have broken a precious vase
those that can only be painted with a one-haired brush
those whose tongues light candles on the fingers of our hands
those that curl their tails
those that refute the Argument from Design, such as bedbugs
    and liver fluke
stupid ones
those that lie still for a while and then run
those whose being makes an unloosenable knot
those that are bored
the good-natured beetles
those such as frogs and snails that are Enlightened beings
humans, born unable to stand
those that are fit to be emblazoned on a flag
mosquitoes
crocodiles
those that should exist – unicorns and mermaids
unacceptable ones, unless we can make a great rational effort
those that cause people to smile – ladybirds, etc.
those that stir in us an erotic feeling
those that are easily broken and yet their kind continues to exist
those that one would like to be – the centaur, the phoenix.

Robert Gray

Kakadu

1.
below skirts of dead leaves
pandanus fray
into 'knock 'im down season'

speargrass fires
burn across the plains
the first clouds of the wet yet to gather

a smashed guano
of insects smears the windscreen
of the red Suzuki cruiser

and birds of prey high in the sky
hover over the souls of bones
bleaching inside the Kakadu gates

2.
the banana plantations
near Humpty Doo burn carefully
filling the sky with smoke

and when we stop to buy mangoes
sunlight has carved wombs into trees
the fruit ripening in late September

at Bark Hut
the emu's copper-blue throat gleams
hard and scraggy as the soil

and like a forest of black cheroots
an acre of sooty-trunked woollybutts
stretches finitely away

3.
Cathedrals of the North:
the termite mounds are silent at matins –
nothing here that Douglas Stewart

did not notice:
the caves of painted hands, those hands
in the black rock, like hands in a grave

here, my son photographs the billboards
– what are you doing? I ask
Not disturbing the wildlife he replies

Kakadu night:
a barn owl swoops our car, swoops again
catching moths in the headlights

Jennifer Harrison

Wallabies

... some memories from somewhere those scattered trees
that straggle of white tree limbs like bleached bones

perhaps a line from someone else or myself
memory of the flattest waters I've ever seen

emerging dreamlike from the low brown skyline
bouquets of white cockatoos bursting from the leaves

out-of-time movement over the dead stubble
what've they been doing? they've been hiding

they've been hiding in the mind, in the body
and then some images of suddenly meeting

that low brown water's thin mirror
as if the crowd of trees signalled to it, or had been

signalling all their lives, building riverine clusters,
building their wandering cicatrice seen from far off –

but when you get there it's the necessary damage
of banks and flooded logs, dried up pools, Toyota paths

nestled spots to fish from the ones safe to swim
flickering shadows hands of them sweeping over the sand

that sense too of clayed ground of earth dust grit pebbles
shards of bark crumbling the crumble and dust of leaves

earth hard with veins of muddy tree roots showing there
wooden dark veins jutting through aged flesh

everywhere the scatter of light from the ground upwards
brilliance of dry dead things shining back in your face

great uplifted spaces glistening with blueness warm air
scent of honeyed fragrant pollens and of less sweet wax

heat smell like some soft linen's invisible cushion
the light threads of native bees, chases of flies

cicadas clicking and humming their electric shavers
a sound system hiddenly installed inside the halfway

bare dancefloor over there between the bottlebrushes
their sawing rhythm nearly as toneless as wooden clacks

but it picks up like an outboard then dies to comes back
saw-toothed that side not noticed now this side here

the great long wave of cicadas breaking like fire
night's burnt firemarks streaked down tree-boles' white flesh:

afternoon's white flesh is the memory of this
the thing which is hidden like a name is hidden

an island which is islanded because it is so far away
because it floats between skylines where distant grey trees

hover above the ground where things appear as if
in appearance they've acted on you they live they breathe

nothing is dead here the spaces between them are
inhabited leaves twigs debris fallen white-anted trunks

slopes rocks grass parrots galahs floating down
in pink streamers again the grey lack of edge

around sprays cream waterfalls of turpentines flowering
in high irrigated air-blue reaches she-oaks aspirant

with their million fingers and amber seed-flowers
spotted gums mottled as grandmothers but with contrasts

of grey brown white and silver as if dressed for a ball
the reds of the king parrot slashing the foliage

with its opening and closing flower as it flies up
vertically to land yes a blinding red and blue male

these flashes of thought these memories now planted
these hard-cased seeds needing fire to sprout these nets

of dirt leaf and twig where ants fossick mason bees sandmine
these laceworks of bark litter and dropped branches

are inland floodwater you wade through to get to land
they're the fuel for the long sweep of the mind's eye

a blanket building up over the worst sterility and death
radiance offers sore bruises earth turns to clay and bakes

an imaginary tide holds blood and featherdown in flight
in place on the edge in the middle in the heart's moment

in the absent space between regions rapidly turned blue
as the ridges stretching west the gulleys sharp as razors

echo after echo after echo of a sound tracking in peaks
till it scratches small shimmers on rocks smoothed by wind

then it lays its long body out there called the west
it's the land scarcely touching the earth swarms of them

it's the land dotted with saltbrush and bush tomato
that twenty mile shadow across the claypan's a fence

which as dusk comes is a lightning-quick snake
momentarily distracting the way they appear

as if from nowhere like sentinels weathered stone
camping in that stubble sunset-toned no like mushrooms

wallabies two of them and then three over there then more
pale half-red underfur letting them melt into late light

alert as the slanting hour's alert to earth cool as wine
then the shriek as they scatter having nursed the air

having known everything as the waking dreamer
knows everything for a scattered instant instantly gone

time's far-sighted body felt beloved and lost in time
the memory of it like the memory of a lover

as familiar as a body curled around yours each day
just like when evaporating inland daybreak starts you wake

Martin Harrison

Braid on Braid

Braid and Max are characters from the 'Peter Henry Lepus in Iraq 2003' sequence in Not Finding Wittgenstein. *Braid, a young journalist interested in environmental geography, has followed Max Strang, an ex-ABC reporter, to Iraq after the fall of Baghdad. Max, who reports for the* Herald *as well as working for a travel organisation, has lured Braid away from his Sydney editor, her former lover. She has been researching the river systems of southern Iraq. They are in the early stages of a love affair, camping in Josh Smith's semi-ruined house in Baghdad.*

Braid decides,
she writes
on thin airmail paper,
she doesn't want
a child yet
with Max – he's too independent
& un-
'family focused'. She doesn't think
he'd make a good father yet,
not
the way he is now:
too much the
unencumbered
    single reporter,
disappearing
by air to Riyadh (*Back in two days*
followed by flight details)
without telling her
why he's going,
    (the absence of his air travel bag,
cryptic as a note with *read me* on it
followed by invisible writing);

then, just talking of taking a trip
to northern Iran –
where the hot springs – & less active   volcanic areas are –
round the east & west ends of the Caspian – which
she wants to write about   & has   talked with him
recently   about wanting to visit
to see how eco-development & tourism
are impacting on the wildlife, & if,
since two thousand,
there's been an increase
in sewerage pollution, in the Caspian,
if measures
are being taken to combat it.
If so, what?
but he hasn't   even asked her
if she wants to come with him.

Perhaps, she, too, needs to grow up
she confides, ending a
letter to
her widowed grandmother out from Mudgee.

Then, taking stock,
seemingly alone in the
semi-ruined house,
feeling slightly sick
& suspecting pre-menstrual tension,
Braid wonders what her chances are
of passing a recruitment office for new, post-Saddam-&-Ba'ath-
Party-appointed, police, on her way
to arrange the letter's posting
to her granny, of ending up:

                       namelessly melded
with an unknown bomber & some equally-unknown-to-her
randomly passing
husbands, fathers, children   & mothers

as depersonalised de-humanised   flecks of bone, blood & flesh
(not like the skinny sheep
her granny routinely drives in the back of a ute
to be illegally slaughtered
& sold in a rural home-made-pie shop in Australia)

but right here   on a Baghdad street.

J.S. Harry

Dark Bird

What do you want with me today, dark bird?
Why are you flying low, beneath that branch?
I know your shadow: you were long since gone,
My killdeer, rough-winged swallow, mourning dove,

Death plays its flute with all your bones, dark bird,
You brood within my nest of breath, dark bird,
Your razor claw is in my eye, dark bird,
Sweet finches are in blossom here, dark bird,

My father's dying now, dark bird, you know,
He feels your shadow now, dark bird, you know,
His bones are hollow now, dark bird, you know,
He's turned to feathers now, dark bird, you know,

Take to another land, dark bird, fly now,
Go snap sweet sunflower souls, dark bird, fly now,
A thousand deaths await you there, dark bird,
Fly fast dark bird fly fast fly past dark bird

Kevin Hart

Climate change: *yugantameghaha*

At the end of every cosmic cycle
at the end of a generation – *yuganta-
meghaha* – clouds congregate
gathering souls for the next *yuga*

cloud breath, soul mist
rasping winds, rattling bones
here come the galloping horses
humans astride their flanks

here come the thundering clouds
breaking the world apart
the Hercules moth climbs every building
rising upwards through 110 floors

scaling the earth to find the moon
that light in the sky through which
he might escape earth's pull
and melt into the inferno of light.

Susan Hawthorne

The words in brackets are from Gaskin's 'A Bud'

for Claire Gaskin

(No anxiety has family)
nowhere else to go to be taken in

(the bleeding palm of an open gate)
the face of the power-point
Whichever way you run you can't escape your lineage
we were told to never lie down not for anyone

(The cup aching for approval)
the leather almost missing the fingers
The sun doesn't betray me it hides

(breasts, money, a baby)
to begin with children have no need for drugs
Forgetting my grandfather's name again
the pushers should have their hands cut off apparently
No one wants to close the door that keeps slamming

(My body not a crime scene)
the last one hundred blows of the feet before the familiar street
i could not play at being a monster

(the silence in the trees is listening to me)
attempting to remember any kind of mistake
The nightly return of the lights in the driveway and footsteps
    coming up the stairs
Learning for the first time that apples can rot

(A wound to the back of the heart)
Driving an old stump into the earth
He came at me sometimes with a spider
bring the White King close to overthrow him

(My lips stuck to the lie as if it were ice)
The smell of stains on the tablecloth and stars outside the
 window
Could not try harder
But in screams begin abilities
Stumbling through straight lines falling off bridges knocking
 on walls
We were exorcised in the yards and neighbours were always nice
The screws getting looser

(Throw your anchor down into the sea of his snoring)
Darkness always light enough to show shadows
surveying the wrecked angles of our room
the clock mocking itself every hour

(the arrhythmia of stifled silence)
putting down the glass like a statement
i could not be small enough
It hurt before it hit

(all the blue rushing through the pinpoint of an iris)
his lips drawn like the line of the horizon
The Long Weekend
Because of you i don't want to be bitter
the sunflower's one eye sees beyond clouds

(breath is happening the rain is happening here there is no
 better)
drought or not most fallen water gets lost

(The pen on the pain)
Sentencing myself first
Precious possessions of self worth
Wanting to turn the sheets inside out
Knowing when not to stop

(as water moves through parting rock)
anyone who ever remembered anything got forgotten

(Let all fall from him)

Matt Hetherington

Egret

It's not even standing at a sensible angle to the river:
beak neither facing downstream
nor into the flow of fish. It's askew, the hulk wedged

the head re-coiled so that
it's slack on the dowdy shelf of itself.
A study in oddball patience, non-expectation.

We'd been talking about the pace of Noh plays
and of the way the ghost or the ghost of a ghost
bears witness: the vantage point being the thing.

But this stillness, so unobserved, seems post-ghost.
Its dream if it has one is way up river,
its own witness, standing indifferent to drama.

Impossible bird! But then
as if suddenly fed up with our spectatorship
it drops, stone-grey, a curtain.

Then an inner wing cleaves to that outer wing
and a long night cloak has fallen –
a twin-panelled shroud.

Majestically erect in attendance upon itself,
sword drawn, its feet are powerfully still
in the river's rushing inks.

Savagely it knit-picks its breast, stretches,
stabs at the autumn sky –
wounding the emptiness over cold waters.

Barry Hill

Waking Happens in Reservoirs

After walking back from Shisendo, the hills up ahead smoking, you sit in the middle room, looking into the garden, the Ottowa River rumbling and rushing down on itself just over there, beside the Imperial Villa, the doves cooing further up the slope. They seem to be in the same place as yesterday and the day before. Maybe they have a nest there, except that it's not the season for nests. Maybe they have taken shelter from the rains, which have been coursing through your sleep for two whole nights. Peace.

These doves, they add to the smoke of Hiei-san.
That mist in their throats, their slow deep music.

Water off wide eaves heals the mind –
wakes you before dawn, dove-tuned.

Water off wide eaves returns to the earth happily –
fat splashes on pebbles in lovely runnels.

A surge plays on and off key, mainly on.
A gurgling wins over words, almost pings

dances down, pocks stone, hums, plucks
little hollows from time like flames.

You soften and sleep, soften and fall back to sleep.
The waking happens in reservoirs of temples.

Barry Hill

an anatomy of birds

You found it in the humus
of emergent things, its
feather skull one hundredth
of its skyborne weight, grey

treasure gone, keel clung to
its breast no longer obliged
to guide and pitch, your fingers,
still with their flesh, decadent

against this picked white, your
density fondling its hollowness,
the cavities that once dissected
light, one feather fixed to its

ladder spine, Jurassic toes coiled
to their fate, your hand defies the
giant's requisite to crush, this fragile
survey of the possibility of flight.

Lia Hills

Capriccio: Spring

On the roadside, burnt orange blossoms in the poinciana.
He says *carnal*, because the colour seems unsupportable
the way their bodies are after fucking, shaken, hollowed out
and tender as the bitter seeds of pomegranates they eat,
but the woman isn't convinced. She looks at him tiredly.
Raw sprays of petals, blood. Both mortal. So what.
He is thinking that over time she has become
very exacting; stubborn, even. Like pine oil. Lime.
And that this seems to have distilled in her body,
the silver ring gleaming on her finger like a shield,
the rosin knot of hair at her neck, and the slightly sour
sheen of sweat building on her cupid's bow that smells,
he thinks, like one of those small, wiry shrubs
that muscle their way out of rock by will. Woody. Resinous.
The youngest of three sisters. Her mother a cellist.
First she is examining the tree, her head still as a stone
curlew, her yellow dress moving vaguely around her knees,
then she is telling him about the thing she saw
in a restaurant in Berlin, or was it Leipzig –
a young man, he must have been early twenties,
unfolding his napkin gingerly and then, swaying
like a praying mantis on a limb, he sat cleaning
his knife and fork over and over, pedantic,
neither looking up nor ordering. At least fifteen
whole minutes, she says, and then a thin old woman
came in and took him away. He tries to imagine
what the story means, whether it's the young man's
compulsion or the grandmother's patience
that matters. No idea. Truth is he hates it –
or not hates it exactly, but is pained when she talks
like this. Man, café, cutlery. Say it plainly.

Clear morning: spring. Black-chinned honeyeaters
threading their nests with grass. Pollen burning
like incense. And the woman behind him – sitting? standing? –
could be anywhere, Prague, Ravenna, the long-faced one
wearing heavy satin in a Ter Bosch or the faithful courtesan
who drinks lime and rose tisane or the Chinese girl
with moon pearls in her ears who scorns the lord
governor's advances and gathers full-blooded mulberries
in a basket of blue silk and cinnamon
wood. Silkworms in the palm, fat flesh, dark juice.
It's hard to say how it begins: you wake one morning,
the doorbell rings, someone's smoking, there's a woman
you meet after night classes for Vietnamese
who talks earnestly about Sudan, she hates novels
but likes the string quintets of Mendelssohn, and you find
yourself watching the way her hands move, languid,
graceful as bamboo fans over the duck curry. Something
happens. She coughs, her hands almost conducting.
We say hunger but mean adoration, single-mindedness:
hand on the heart, wet palms, a cool drumming
in the stomach. It's late. I don't care, she says, I'm not tired.
Clear morning: spring. A man has been sitting on a balcony
for hours, the cat sprawled beside him, eating loquats and reading
about Dürer's watercolours. The little owl's tailfeathers
remind him of something, dry and papery as nutmeg,
translucent over the ink. A woman's hair, maybe. Rust,
or that wet-foal tint of chestnut. What is it? Then she runs in
wearing a pair of yellow and blue-striped sneakers, radiant;
there's a lizard eating a cricket, they watch it silently,
then they are laughing, he's not sure about what, but he likes
the way she looks at him afterwards, almost ruefully.
Clear morning: spring. Birds preening meticulously on a wire.

Green emperors hovering uncertainly. And a woman
walking under a tree, it could be towards or away
from him – impossible to tell at this distance –
her dress is yellow, flimsy, but the colour of the petals
is the important thing, they are falling, lacquer red, ember,
cadmium, the woman is still walking, and the wind
rises like the flash of fire under a dragonfly's wing.

Sarah Holland-Batt

For Nina

I. AFTER MEN

Much I could say, said the seeress,
of the gods' choice of end.

Odin shall speak with Mimir's head.
Brothers shall fight, cousins shall bed,

killing kinship the other way.
No man will be spared by another,

which is to say no man will spare himself.
Hard is it in the world!

The giantesses shall flee, their big thighs
slipping below the horizon,

the light with them.
An axe age, a sword age (things

shall be split), a wind age, a wolf age (before
the world sinks).

II. Before Men

Time takes too much time! you sang as we took
to the wind, pulling our hair from our mouths

and breathing out air still spindrift.
In the two remaining greys of last light

the storm came in on the king tide's back;
by morning the jetty would be broken to bits.

That night we stood at the jetty's clinging root-end
and ran. The waves broke over both sides

to make us an arbour of threat and glisten;
we jumped the loosed planks that clacked

in retarded joy *sea! sea!* as we reached the sprig-end.
You clutched your crotch in happy fear

and lost your hat. The railings were all gone:
we were standing on a platter, offered up.

L.K. Holt

Meteor IV at Cowes, 1913

Sydney in spring. Tonight you dine alone.
Walk up the Argyle Cut to Argyle Place
And turn left at the end. In there you'll find
Fish at the Rocks: not just a fish-and-chip joint
But a serious restaurant, with tablecloths
And proper glassware. On the walls, a row
Of photographs, all bought as a job lot
By a decorator with a thoughtful eye:
Big portraits of the racing yachts at Cowes
In the last years before the First World War.
Luxurious in black and white as deep as sepia,
The photographs are framed in the house style
Of Beken, the smart firm that held the franchise
And must have had a fast boat of its own
To catch those vivid poses out at sea:
Swell heaving in the foreground, sky for backdrop,
Crew lying back on tilting teak or hauling
On white sheets like the stage-hands of a classic
Rope-house theatre shifting brilliant scenery –
Fresh snowfields, arctic cliffs, wash-day of titans.
What stuns you now is the aesthetic yield:
A mere game made completely beautiful
By time, the winnower, whose memory
Has taken out all but the lasting outline,
The telling detail, the essential shadow.

But nothing beats the lovely, schooner-rigged
Meteor IV, so perfectly proportioned
She doesn't show her size until you count
The human hieroglyphs carved on her deck
As she heels over. Twenty-six young men
Are present and correct below her towers
Of canvas. At the topmost point, the apex
Of what was once a noble way of life
Unquestioned as the antlers in the hunting lodge,
The Habsburg eagle flies. They let her run,
Led by the foresail tight as a balloon,
Full clip across the wind, under the silver sun,
Believing they can feel this thrill for ever –
And death, though it must come, will not come soon.

Clive James

When Years Take the Stars Away

If you're reading this in one-hundred-million,
two-thousand and seven A.D., that is, after all the stars
have inched away, taking their tails of light with them,
far off to where the universe strikes a light against
what, at the time of writing, has no dimension, the timeless
place that time is coming to, I want to tell you
that here – right now – the sky is prinked
with nebulae in clusters and symposium,
the light is mostly white, so you get the true idea of blackness
and the abundance is such that it presses infinities
into the foreheads of children lying safe in their beds at night,
and those who can get out from the cities
and take the time to sit outside, make up elaborate
stories, concerning these embroideries of starlight, and if
a meteorite rushes, burning, into the earth's air,
wonderment bubbles up, into this strange satisfaction
which might be happiness. I want you to know, as you sit
reading this on your black and starless planet
that you should not find that blank
blanket of night a reason to believe that stars do not exist,
the galaxies, the Milky Ways and the jewel of Magellan's Clouds,
still shine and burn abundant in distant orbits.

Carol Jenkins

Black Cockatoo: *Calyptorhynchus funereus*

The dab of yellow in each black tail
and at the side of the head
is an anointed aggression
It's said they once flew too close to heat or ice
to pure extinction
Their ancient task – to blacken the sun's remnant flares
Of the birds, they alone survived, so anger is their afternote
See these fanning Majas
serrate the do-gooder sky
See the dead-eyed, helmeted leader bid
the pine needles rush upwards to receive their *Ur*-adolescence
Not for them to be the bird of Hope
to mourn the marshlands of Baghdad
A thousand seed-gutted cones bomb the dry earth
The stripped, cratered hills will be theirs
no matter how we foul them, no matter how we die

A. Frances Johnson

The Wind-up Birdman of Moorabool Street

The wind-up bird ticks
the real bird chirps
the man speaks
You have never known what makes you tick, chirp or speak, I say
You turn malachite eyes
to grim truths as to happy
oblivious to infinitesimal shifts
in your fine bone mass
the cold rush of blood
hurling robin-red
along the miniature flight paths of your body
Each day the hurl is pinstriped into submission
Caw-caw-caw can even sound conversational in some situations
Your flight instincts are made over into 'acceptable departures'
The downy sleight of your neck and head
helps others avoid perceptions of hairlessness
the repetitions of your sharp focused hands
their deft studied motions over a briefcase full of seeds
– these are all good
the best possible excuses for not speaking
Darling creature, you almost never flutter
You *almost* pull it off
this blood masquerade
Until the rains come and the worms tessellate the garden
Then the wind-up bird ticks within and without
and in the grey morning light
I see you in your business suit
bent stiff-legged over your prey beneath the elms
singing at the top of your voice
the car alarms sounding dully on Moorabool Street

A. Frances Johnson

Oh, Sydney

What does autumn tell us
apart from the passing of seasons
and crows sitting on power lines
as trains weary their way in the slower mornings,
those mornings that aren't necessary
but cooler, while the news elects other avenues of feeling,
about devastation, which is difficult under the blue,
the azure feeling, when your clothes seem sharper
tailored to crispness, and to the needs of meetings,
all those people who think, somehow, there's something to say.
What is there to say, this breathlessness
won't uncover any other feeling than change
which you can breathe as smoke, or a letter
that comes from another city you might like
to change into, but why, this place is more than enough,
its harbours, and rivers, and the planes above,
constants in a changeable present, among
leaves and a daylight moon you could trace
in a drawing of your day, there's that rabbit's outline
on the surface of something other than the earth.
You make a story or a trace of it
but it only lasts while you look up, while along the street
you can't find a taxi or any way home that's without effort.

Argument sucks up the day hours and the night
should be free of this, but along the harbour walls
there is still doubt about who owes you the way
when here is millionaire's row, the swish,
the balconies full of none other than ourselves,
those selves with more money than we could pocket
though we dream, looking up, missing the light,
the vacant, the way out, past flyovers and factories
to a kind of ordinary, where the dog with three legs
has wondered in the dog way, where a door might let out
onto the grass, for relief, and so near the river
once full of refuse, now almost desirable and making
a way past mangroves and mess to the bay
under flight paths and stars that have stared at the sea
but not quite in the smothered way the new century lends
to strands of time and night, and the call you make
not from a machine but a passion, that old call
you make from the restless body which somehow represents
the heart, the centuries, the wish and futures,
the faint smell of diesel, eucalypt, sandstone and tar.

Jill Jones

Chased Seas Urge

In the mangroves, we avoid the shade black with swarming sandflies. I know I should tell you. I should say, I know I would tell you. But the sun is going down and the tide is coming fast and invisible as fear. Swallowing the partings. The shadows are growing longer and we have to walk further into the water to avoid the bites that will itch for days. Your back is covered in black flies hitching a ride. I follow the wake left by your strong legs. I am strong too, but smaller, the sea has a hold on more of me so I try to use my cupped hands like paddles. I have that curiosity, what happens if I let go? Give way to the pull, go with the flow. I mean you hear stories. Behind the island is a whirlpool, the old man told me last night. He told it better than I remember it. You turn to smile and that knowing is closer than the shadows. My toes feel the sharp roots in the mud, more tiny cuts to keep clean. There is a deep waterhole, more an undersea landhole here, somewhere, we fished it yesterday until the turtles snapping the lines won, competition, not a battle and I cried to think of the hooks in their stomachs. Then you said 'sshh, there's enough salt water here'. The Bardi woman came with a spear and caught one real quick and we shared her family's meal. My mind is there now with the turtles and the fish we didn't eat. We need to hurry. Creature and creature relocate now, at dusk. Some will eat each other. Soon it will come down to a choice between the bites and currents that will sweep us out fast to sea. Discomfort will win.

Amanda Joy

Thoughts in the Middle of the Night

All is dark but for the greenish glow
Of the bedside clock radio
It's 3 a.m. – here they come again
Just like they've done before
First there's one and then a couple more
Like little birds perching on a wire
And soon there's a gathering
A crooning restless choir
Of thoughts in the middle of the night

You toss and turn – 3.45
When little things magnify
Lists uncrossed, chances lost
A conversation gone awry
Now they're lining up – all these old mistakes
You're looking back at the sad parade
Warnings you chose not to hear
Calling now loud and clear
But too late! In the middle of the night

5 a.m. – you haven't solved a thing
You're right back where you started from
And they just won't go away
They have come to play
These thoughts – until the break of day!

Paul Kelly

One More Tune

Night is turning into morning
This shindig's winding down
The cops have been and the cops have gone
Somebody didn't like our sound
Now all this fuss has come down to just us
Singing soft inside a room
Won't you stay now?
Let's play one more tune

Martin's sleeping, we won't wake him
Nothing could do now
He and Ruby've sure had some doozies
But never such a row
Blame it on the bottle
Or blame it on the moon
Oh, come on, stay with me
And play with me one more tune

Close we huddle to keep warm
So frail our candle, so strong the storm

I can't do this on my own
Make the sounds that make me swoon
Please stay a while
Make me smile with one more tune
Every cup, every glass is empty
If you go now it'll be too soon
Won't you stay here
And play one more tune?
Come on, won't you stay
And slay me with one more tune

Paul Kelly

Leonard Cohen in Concert, Hunter Valley, January 2009

The vineyard is pinstriped with light and shade,
though shade is scarce. To the south, a fire
will soon become a killing furnace yet here,
on the last day of the first month of the year,
the news is good. The Triffids play to all
but empty grass. Paul Kelly's quiet set calls
the faithful out from under tents and trees.
When he leaves the stage it's almost dark.
After the break, Leonard Cohen and his band
walk out to a standing ovation. It's not the crowd
but what it brings and receives that matters.
The man who wears an Armani suit to sweep
the floor and do his washing doffs his fedora,
smiles, then steps into the opening chords
of 'Dance Me to the End of Love'. Nearby
someone is sobbing. A man holds his daughter up
as if to receive a blessing. When he lets her down,
the bottle of Ballantines we'd smuggled in
is kicked from my hand as I fill a glass. I pour
another as the band goes into 'The Future'.
Cohen's sense of style and old world manners
are evident and in abundance. Often,
as the 'Shepherd of the Strings', Javier Mas
is soloing on the banduria, sitting on the edge
of a red armchair, Cohen kneels before him,
hat in hand, watching respectfully.
This gesture is afforded everyone, and often.
'There Ain't No Cure for Love' sets the tone
and spirit for the night. I overhear a woman
say she'd been with him in London.

He prefaces songs with stories of depression,
meditation and how, after years of drugs
and study, *cheerfulness just kept on breaking through.*
After 'Bird on the Wire', in the first intermission,
I walk through the crowd and listen. On the hill
it seems too quiet for a concert, with people
standing around as if trying to remember
something they'd meant to say, or do.
The stage is like a scallop shell, with dark blue
screens and Cohen's own design: a heart
with a hummingbird in flight above it.
Leonard Cohen knows how reclusiveness
and shunning fellowship affect the spirit.
At the end of 'If It Be Your Will' and before
'I Tried To Leave You', he offers his blessings
to those returning with friends and family
and to those going home to their solitude.
Then it's over. At 74 he won't be back.
Walking to the bus, I see an old friend from Wagga.
He's off somewhere with the night in his head
and I will not interrupt him.

Anthony Lawrence

The Burden & the Wing

I went to where belief had said
the dirt on love had been laid down
& turned & aired for companion planting
or some random choice of seed
thrown out to take & flourish.
Belief was wrong. I found beauty
in the detail as when, from the throat
of a courting frigate bird, we see
the sexed-up membrane bloom
& fall, but not the bird itself.
Belief had raised a screen of smoke
or dust before, & I had entered it
in faith, & found betrayal talking filth
behind its hand when the screen came down.
Yet still I go, trusting in the blood
of what we think we ought to know.
I once believed I could tell my love
from the scent a body makes
in twinned desire. I was wrong.
The giant cuttlefish understands
for the season of its life, that sex
a colour-coded time & place
& then forgets & dies. Hovering,
its cuttlebone pocketed with air,
it looks into a diver's mask
& sees itself, the reef gone to neon,
its three hearts snare-drumming
green blood behind its eyes
& then it's over, where attraction
hangs its mandibles & slime.

A man & woman will hear
each other's names, & belief
will raise its knife & glass & they
will feast on intimacy, the underside
of wisdom, the torn pelt of grief
already over them as they say
Here & now & Oh my love You are
& We believe & Can this be enough?
What happens when the curious animal
inside us dies? It takes a hand
inside a hand to bring it back,
& breathing hard we try & fail, & try
to guide ourselves to where,
unassisted, we can stand & shine.
We fall in love, pregnant, prey
& victim to, asleep, under, over,
away & down, & when belief falls
we are left without connecting language
for what happens next.
Direction has no sense, & inarticulate
we lose our way. *Save yourselves*,
the little tern spells out
in headland semaphore, & we do, again,
alone & never getting used to it.
Falter & cry, good human, & remember –
wherever we are can be the healing ground
in love's geography. We come & go
for solitude, family, for walks when dusk
lets out its fan, & under cover there
we give ourselves the time to change,
lighting the touch paper of renewal.

We travel, loving one, yet knowing
how desire for another has been ours
& most likely will again be ours,
we move from heat to fire in the open
field between devotion & alarm.
We fan the flames or will the wind
to change direction, the rain to fall,
the new love to be of its time & end.
But it remains, & wreckage is what
it often leaves – wilful, seismic, raw.
A shift of plates along a line of faults.
Sparks & scars, the weathervane
throws its voice & we follow
compass points to find it.
Lie down with me the ebb tide says,
under its outgoing breath.
We've no defence for the kinds
of influence that heal. Some fight it,
& for their black resolve take
abandonment, reclusiveness, opening
their chests, unpacking boxes of ants,
listening to wind & water, birds & fish.
A bathroom's acoustics perfect
& archive the sound of weeping,
although mirrors should be avoided.
The bedroom is commonplace,
& grief is expected there.
Even the shadows are welcoming.
Shrines to the family of five beside
the highway, ash from the clapped hands
of a daughter at the Gap –
the end of love is another kind of death,
& being alone is what it's about.

Grief puts down its hat & stands aside
to let time ply its long, essential trade.
Saying goodbye is a flute stop
untroubled by breath & fingertip,
though lines of music still bleed out
between the hours of light & light.
If belief has a face, it is that of anyone
who has said I love you with all the hurt
it takes to say I love you. If belief
has a voice, it is the sound
of a secret breaking down on the tongue.
Tonight, on some old player
with a blunt needle, it's the static
in 'Don't Give Up'. I believe
in all the voices I am & have been,
but that doesn't mean I understand them.
It's what we hear when we put
our critical heads to sleep & learn
from imagination. There are no words
for the ways we respond to the sex
in a glance or the kindness in dismissal.
Belief is the burden & the wing.
It takes what it takes & nothing more
to carry it.

Anthony Lawrence

Heat Wave, Melbourne—
Hottest Day on Record since 1855

Snorkelling a sunken platform three feet deep
    south of Ricketts Point,
        coralline, in various shades of lime

some white with death
    stand out in a field of glow weed
        and sea lettuce.

A transparent shrimp
    treads water– its swimmerets
        on fast-flipper– crunches a piece

of eel grass with maxilliped-snatch,
    does a ninety-degree shift,
        drops the fragment,

then return-butts a dark-mouthed conniwink
    as if mad
        with reckoning.

That's when I notice
    an entire family of conniwinks
        bumping into each other.

A smooth pebble crab, its swollen claws
    embracing the base of clump grass,
        holds tight as a boat's wake

    churns sand
        and gusts everything
            sideways. Then an

unidentified mollusc,
    with its own moss garden
        on its back– has learnt

to trust camouflage– manoeuvres
    in strap weed without
        freezing-frame. Easy to

float for hours in this kelp meadow
    – the heat above –
        where

orange winged spider-wasps
    oddly emerge
        from coastal heath

and hover sea-surface
    for anything liquid. Where
        cormorants gather with no need

for wing-drying. Where
    crested terns fly lower
        than yesterday. Where

a fly drops out of the sky
    landing dead
        on my lap.

Michelle Leber

The Animals

A 'domesticated bearded dragon $400'
is not my idea of an animal companion
A calf asleep on a double bed, perhaps,
or a hare with long ears
crouched under a mahogany sideboard,
thumping the floor.
Or a koala that climbed up a four-poster bed
surprising a seventeen-year-old in her nightie.

They were here before us – the animals –
and we were once them.
Without understanding we watched the sunrise
and the coming of night,
registered the changing of seasons
and dew on leaves that brushed our flanks.
We, the animals,
knew feelings, had a memory,
exchanged sounds and visual cues,
but did not know
what came before
or ask what was to come.

A neighbour sleeps with a wombat in her bed,
and her husband sleeps on the veranda.
Kangaroos watch TV through her sitting-room window.

Bottle-fed joeys get osteoporosis
if the composition of the milk isn't right.
The females make better companions.
With shy brown eyes
they hop along beside you
as you collect mail from the gate at dusk.

We were once them,
and now are their custodians.
They know we are different
and their eyes tell us to keep our promise.

Bill came home after a fortnight away
Pot plants had been kicked off the veranda,
there was an awful smell,
and the front door was ajar.
Inside the house
chairs were overturned,
papers and cushions trampled on floors,
and in the bathroom,
wedged against the washbasin,
her putrid flesh held together by hide,
Twinkle, a pony.
A tractor winched the body out.

Geoffrey Lehmann

Rain in March

Rain comes in the night,
Unexpectedly, puttering on the roof,
Plashing in the street, then raging,
Sounding to submerge the house
In lashing scuds, with dull roars
Of thunder.
          Day dawns
Misty, with driving rain still,
Water dripping from eaves, spotting,
Spattering through foliage. It follows
A constant rhythm, sometimes fast
With drumming, splashing fury,
Hammering, lashing at windows,
Then slow, slipping back
To a whisper – a speaking rain,
Regularity in irregularity –
With metallic, single drops dripping
In echoing down-pipes – perfect
Stillness with motion still.

Life contracts about the house –
Just outside, gum leaves, wattle leaves,
Glisten richly through the droplets.
Dull brown earth shines
With the silver showers, as runnels
Start and flow clear through the beds,
To swash out over paths. In the house
Papers curl, carpets, curtains
Unlock smells.
          Cloud presses down
All through the day, as the rain
Drizzles and sputters on and on.

Each near hill wears
A white, fluffy shroud.
                    At dusk
The far murk gathers and darkness
Falls, sizzling with insect-song –
Chirping crickets and autumn peepers
Trilling – with carolling of magpies
And currawongs, and a brief clamour
Of cockatoos.
                    In the muted darkness
The front passes, single drops
Spitting from a matt black sky –
Rain has washed through the world,
A faint, cool wind lifts
Branches heavy with wet leaves.

John Leonard

'We believe in killing idiots'*

to Mark Boulos; for Stephen Carino

On the pearly Niger river
metallic Nigerian delta
gunboats' guerrillas
'believe in killing idiots'
     make war, that's *war*
on corporations'
oil rigs –
platforms raised
like metal skirts
above the sea,
wading in riches
dark, in deep water
Congratulations on the footage
In bright primary colours
     uniformed traders
rev the floor
at the Mercantile Exchange,
speculate in futures
ever more loudly
Congratulations on this mediation
Between two screens
     our I-senses melt into air;
Nigerian fighter on one screen
murmurs:
'We believe in killing idiots'
Chicago traders on the other
shout in code
ever more loudly
Congratulations on this footage

god Egbisu
loves the fighters
maybe the market loves
Chicago traders
ever more loudly
speculating on futures;
    oil does what oil does
in the Nigerian delta
as gunboats' guerrillas patrol
Congratulations on the mediation
We sit between screens
taking it all in
oil rigs penetrate the sky the sea
like compass needles
always pointing north;
no spillover profits
along the equator
    for delta villagers
on the wrong side;
traders at the Mercantile Exchange
reach climax
cacophony
This world these futures
    ours as we melt into air
Congratulations

Kerry Leves

---

* Based on Mark Boulos' video-installation *All That Is Solid Melts Into Air* (2008), featured in the Sydney Biennale 2008, at Cockatoo Island, Sydney Harbour.

The Egret

> *Otherworldly, celibate –*
> *oh, manicured object – you're some*
> *righteous sect's uncharred lamp wick.* —Judith Beveridge

She holds the wick of her neck in place
as she steps slowly down the canal.
I cannot help but watch: how she stops

to nail an invisible fish and pincers
my heart. In this morning's grey gloom,
she is a pale rag dropped

by the water's edge then moves off
into bird again. Whenever I see an egret
I want to ask how it keeps so white

after days spent sifting through mud
and stormwater. She is a snip of paper,
a perfect template, all colour chanted out.

Column of precision, she knows just how
to disturb her world: each gesture an example
of economy, each day a bead of attention.

In the mandibles of pause, I'll imagine
a place where egrets are common as water:
in public parks and suburban gardens –

city streets even. Some nights I dream
all the earth's candles; blazing
their thousands on temple floors,

swung in lanterns, set loose on paper boats
in the darkness. They could be lit souls
    of lost egrets.

All night they burn.
By morning there is nothing to confess.

Debbie Lim

Fred's Farm

yes this is a field of gunmetal glinting like weather
an entire ecology of dead thistles mapping a drought
barbs pain dull remembering poisons of beestings and
the skull-eye fits perfectly a climbing stick found hillside.
let's take a photo here of the air's texture looking
down into damwater figure out some key property of
atomic nature the push of things against another. let
no one say that sheep can't really move if encouraged
when it's a distance issue the soundlessness is affecting
as a cinematic device. this dog resembles more closely a
seal than say a different dog and really the same is elsewhere
too. owls pocket into roofy line-drawings I'm
imagining that everything is a sketch or a story told
hundreds of times at the dinner table. (months ago
on saying I was interested in oral histories I was made
to feel oversexed and dead-keen on performing fellatio.)
rhubarb is a barometer of the times, heirloom parsleys
grow into mad reunions, tomatoes hang on tho pecked
into pumice. predictably all the wool smells of dinner
farmdogs bray fig trees are irrelevant bowsers like delta

Astrid Lorange

Even in the Dark

Even in the dark
the leaves are still

falling – it's a steady smattering now –
dark on dark they

drop through moony shadows
and into crisp, earth-smelling banks:

[meanwhile, we sleep,
turning like planets in the strangeness of

deep dreaming] –
still, the leaves carpet field, roads

and the quiet floor of the woods;
they fill the lengthening night,

whispering of things fallen
and falling, of what sighs

and subsides, of what bides its time,
breathing slow into the long cold of winter,

all in calm readiness for the onset
of small things –

say, a chink of pale light,
the shift and slip of change.

Rose Lucas

Twenty-five Unbroken Bottles of Champ

after The Australian and New Zealand List of Vessels Lost, Missing or Taken from Active Service 1874–1949 *by Peter Taylor*

7 *Alert*s in 38 years / wrecked, foundered or broke-up / 1 cutter / 2 ketches / 1 brigantine / 2 of 3 S.S.-es sunk / 3 years apart off Nambucca Heads / the other off Cape Schanck

/ 2 schooners / tonnage capacity mutual at 47 / both ports of registry / Melbourne / shared birth year / 1876 / each dubbed *Glengarry* / both wrecked in Vic / even the good grace of 16 years between glubs /

Marco Polo / a wonder of Launceston / condemned / age 32 in its namesake slip / 29 tonnes this cutter hauled / never did it wander / afar from Launceston /

1848 / Sydney / the *Lass of Gowrie* nimble her tonnage max a firm 17 / aged 49 / in the registry / her only noted particular ... 'missing for years' /

of the 5 *Hercules* / number 3 in age / dismantled in Brisbane / also at age 47 / sold as parts / register closed / 895 tonnes it could threaten / no more

6 *Magic*s / registered Kiwis / or loyal Sydneysiders / 5 broke or wrecked / here or there / in 25 years / the tiniest *Magic* / an entry / final in registry / cancelled / 17 tonne lugger / June / 1920

/ another Brisbane gal in straights / built, 1853 / torched alive / *Louisa Maria* / natives of The Whitsundays / aged 25 / atypically warm that / August /

the *Mystery* / dynamited / 1906 in Lyttleton / a ketch

{*130*}

/ of little importance save that it took 2 years to blow / still registered active / 1908 /

Adelaide / cutter *Surprise* / sunk in collision / 1917 / location unknown /

Erected to proudly move 81 tonnes of what-have-yous / at 21 / Auckland / wrong turn / disgracing itself into houseboat / S.S. *Pitoitoi* / 52 tonnes the lesser a craft / 1939 / erased from the books / gone

Kent MacCarter

Clare and Paris

Clare Collins woke up in the Paris Hilton. Paris
Hilton was on the TV. Fox News, having disastered
on Iraq, retrained its sites
on Paris Hilton, more in its scope, but its
obscene joy at her suffering, her crying for
her mother, filled Clare with horror.
           The hotel
was as smooth, clean and confident with light
as Paris herself once. The city itself, however,
seemed to Clare the world's most terrible.
She had thought at first it would be like
a metaphor for herself, who had killed
her younger siblings as a child, in what
she was forced to acknowledge had been
a type of revolution. The Catacombs of skeletons,
now tourist attractions, might be like
the way the haunted have to treat their lives
and deaths as over-crowded commodities. Poor
Paris the woman in prison reminded
Clare of grief. At an early age, Clare
had been warned by George Jeffreys that any
emotion she showed about her crimes – especially
remorse – would seem obscene, so she'd
just shrugged her soul back into the normal,
felt the usual things about most things, with some
relief. And one of the more normal things she always
felt was grief. Paris the city was grief,

                         so grey
and sparkling in its rigid overfocus.
Grief had made Clare careless with her life
if still organising others with that other
big-sisterly carefulness in grief. It seemed as if
her dead flocked beneath her wings
upholding her in danger and she never
cared at all if they should let her fall
to be with them again.
                         But now she left the Hilton
and found the right address. Where suddenly
was fire:
real fire not metaphor danced up
about the old hotel become a refuge
for women and their children from abuse.
Clare was here because the Human Rights
unit she represented had followed up that
Amnesty report condemning maltreatment
of women in France. Perhaps some angry
husband had heard that she was visiting.
                    A crowd
below watched and videoed but no one
appeared on the landing above. Was
the woman in 32 trapped alive waiting?
Whole as usual only in a crisis,
Clare climbed the fire escape. No one
seemed to see her. I have been a ghost
since I was nine, she thought, in terror. Jeffreys
in her head accused her of melodrama. The metal
was hot but the flames were uneven:

sometimes mountainous then skirting
back wider like a pack of wolves. Clare
knew to focus on the horizon, if one
were scared of heights. The Eiffel
Tower obsessed the horizon. The window
to 32 was open. Inside, a woman
was tied to a couch and a baby shrieked. Clare
crept in and untied the lady's washing line
from her arms. The lady quietly rubbed
the blood back as Clare led her out onto
the fire escape, holding the baby, which
breathed now quickly, like a kitten. The crowd
at the bottom of the stairs for some reason
assumed the women lived together. The lady,
who looked like Paris Hilton: fair, fragile, calm
and childlike in inviting conversation,
said, 'I'm Sophie,' politely. Clare asked,
'Do you want to tell the police?', was relieved
when Sophie said, 'You bet', in careful English.
The wolves of flame were rushing at the roof now.
One heard their howl and then the sirens.
Clare swayed giddily and in her head Jeffreys
said by now she should be used to conflict.
Get back, she smiled, old super-ego, you.

With Sophie and the baby,
walking back in the Paris of Sarkozy, this
Bastille Day when he had just refused
to grant the traditional Amnesty in prisons,
Clare said, 'The only really beautiful parts
of Paris are the new concrete suburbs.
They remind me of Mt Druitt: small
trees in grouted tubs and that same eerie
green tinge light has on long concrete malls.'
She texted Jeffreys: 'Darling, as you know,
quite practically, one can't save anyone
at all if one is saving one's own soul.'

Jennifer Maiden

Memory & Slaughter

I. Chickens

I was four or five years old.
My sister, sixteen years older than me,
was at Teachers' College. She worked
Saturdays delivering uncooked,
plastic-wrapped chickens to businesses in town.
She would drive a small, silver-coloured van,
like something from a cheap science-fiction.

We lived in 'the hills'. The farm down the road
gave me a cat I called Tabby. One day
my Scottish mother saw a kangaroo hop
past our house, down the dirt driveway, and
into the paddock across the road.
Next door's guinea fowl occasionally
appeared in our yard, and we would chase them away.

I sometimes went with my sister to deliver
chickens. I can't remember how many times.
It may have been often, it may have been twice.
People in shops would ask if she was
my mother. Or perhaps she was only asked this
once, and that memory now repeats, like
a stone skipping across bright water.

One Saturday the owners of the chicken farm
had slept in. Inside a shed my sister and I watched
as chickens were forced, one at a time, head-
first into large steel funnels fixed upon the wall,
   where
they were beheaded. There was blood and noise.
The chickens' bodies were then placed
into something that looked like a washing machine.

I was told by someone that this machine removed
the feathers. Perhaps I saw this happen, too. I don't
remember. I felt strange, and my sister suggested we
   wait
in the silver van for the chickens to be ready.
After delivering chickens we would usually stop at a
   deli
where my sister would buy me a ham sandwich
wrapped in wax paper, and a cold drink.

But most of this I don't remember. There are gaps.
I don't remember delivering the chickens that day, or
if I had my sandwich and drink. I remember
only my mother berating my sister that night
for letting me see what I had seen, which is now
an imperfect memory that does not skip,
but merely hangs, nauseous, in the space of a
   doorway.

II. A Memory

I almost forgot to tell you
how on the fly-over
to the freeway yesterday

I saw something reddish
on the road, and for a
second or maybe two struggled

to make it out – a child's
soft toy dropped from a car,
a heavy piece of clothing,

the remains of some road kill.
But it was worse. At ninety
kilometres an hour I registered

a fox, shockingly doglike, on its
side, a back leg working hard.
At which point I passed the animal,

and (I was calculating) so had four
other cars in the same moment.
The vehicles, the road and the

guardrails became brutally
improper, and memory (so I thought)
fixed the fox in an animal hell

of bright sky, tarmac and
monstrous noise. A
deathlessness.

III. Whaling Station

In my primitive childhood
the Cheynes Beach Whaling Station
in Frenchman Bay, just outside Albany,

was operational and open to tourists.
My memory gives up very little.
How, out of the dark ocean,

did they find the ocean-coloured bodies of
living whales to turn into pieces? What mysterious
industry was there to turn them into

those pieces? Flenser and Hookman
worked the blubber, while Saw Man and his
steam-driven saw cut the whales' heads to pieces

small enough to fit into the cookers that
were worked by Digester Operator. It
took two men to straighten the harpoons.

Any ambergris found in a whale was sent
to Scotland for refining. But I don't
remember any of this. I just remember that

as we watched from the distance, my father
or brother taking photographs, the vast smell
offered an unimaginable and unrelenting intimacy

of disgust. The equipment was not subtle,
though devious and effective enough. We could
not watch for long, though probably long enough to be

told that the whales' oil, once refined, was used
for special purposes including cosmetics, fine
machinery and watch mechanisms.

From the gift shop we bought
a piece of tooth which, now slightly
yellowed, sits in my parents' bookcase.

The station then must have had about four
or five years left in it, closed down as it was
in 1978 by the rising cost of fuel oil.

David McCooey

Rock Fishing

for my mother

You used to fish off rocks
under whiskered cliffs
where crabs eyed me sideways
clicking like mice bones.

I watched your skill
with knife and knot,
your toughened skin
stained with gut.

I peered in pools
gummed with limpets,
anemones tugged my fingers
like blissful newborns.

We had the salt and wind,
the gulls poised on updraughts
and the far reach
from beach to open sea.

Now you cast
off weathered planks,
turn your eager eye
to the rocks, alert
for the sign of a taut line
a glittering catch, a run of kings.

Our reflections shudder
as the bait dances below.

Susan McCreery

To Peter Rabbit in the Night

for Christopher Eichler

We're outmatched by darkness –
the night unrolls and unrolls
and we *see* them, the rabbits,
hurtling into the charcoal atmosphere,
flashing their incandescent
cottontails behind them. Those tails
a last flashing code from the outskirts
of it all. They're pelting,
open-mouthed, into nothing.
And we're left here, Peter: our heads
poked dreamily out of the warren,
ardent wonderers under the stars.
They say that soon it won't only be rabbits.
– Soon rivers and geese, whales
and hilltops will follow, trailing
the sun and her acolytes until
the cosmos ends our archaeology of light.
And then, Peter, as gravity fails you and me,
our small wonder will briefly mingle
in the emptying sky.

Kate Middleton

The Latter Shall Prevail

In the event of daylight
your body becomes sun, pestle sharp
dream peony

I crawl to you in russet green
my simple math
a chord kept by tender sluts

In the event of agreement
cantabile monarchs flicker abed, garden
spirals spruce

Colour to the laurel.
I blink, the winged creatures gone
upon the laurel limb

In the event of renovation
they chop down gums, sappy flesh
pale and grave

A wolf's blue eye
possessed by human closure, bloody fur
stuck to my fingers

In the event of ecology
the enchantment of property shrieks
poppies, mere nature

Descends into decoration,
a pile-up in winter, angelic weather
crenelating anonymous cathedrals

In the event of false sorrow
estranged but enchanting, cross & recross your mouth
your naked province of power

Two hands, blown sistrum
courting a seminal fancy, most valuable lover
held to the light

In the event of *chestnut, oak, boredom*
the dead season swells into wolves
salt, rooftops glistening

Light angled highlights fault
mysterious & private, each eclipse
equivalent to shit

In the event of technique
shards of water, obligatory guns
perfumed grace

I am happy to die for each shade of whiteness, witness
mortal lingering
in *hedges, humans, horrible dogs*

In the event of anticipation
empire's lucid contour
embroiders over underworld

A tally clod by distant oxen
free fall forests
afternoon orange

In the event of conjecture
enormous hedgerows socket tomorrow
neon marrow, lunar flavour

Only wolves
golden eyes
yawl acumble snow

In the event of darkness
uncommon sirens soothsaw poetics,
thumbprints

calibrate night,
lightning or carbon sky, yon skin,
the latter shall prevail.

Peter Minter

Birdwatching during the Intervention

As soon as we stop we hear them
'didyougetdrunk? didyougetdrunk? didyougetdrunk?'

A gentle waterfall of sound
sometimes close and insistent
mostly a little way off.

As I lie on red sand
crisscrossed with insect, bird, mice, lizard tracks,
whole new stories I can't read every morning,

it's little showers of orange-beaked finches that visit.
'Nyii-nyi, nyii-nyi, nyii-nyi'
they chatter urgently in Pitjantjatjara.

I walk along the vermilion dune
a lone human footprint
around tangles of white flowers.

Singing honeyeaters fly quietly
between scraggy trees
babblers complain loudly in gullies

til I head off across the plain
harsh and glittery in the afternoon
with thousands of little shiny stones

dark and mysterious in the long lake of shadow
as I return from the second dune at dusk –
quails rocketing off at my feet –

and we finally see,
like this is the old days
when whitefellas were few,

one car go past
on the track along the swale
where we're camped.

By the time we leave
I learn it's in the shoulders of the dunes, the sound,
in the dead bushes from the big fire a few years ago.

The large, brown shapes of wedgebills
their cheeky crests
disappear as I get closer

like they're telling me
you can't just look
and expect to see
in this country.

Meg Mooney

hush

often chloroform undertones in the banana-scented
musics of the street some more cigarettes splice
your fingers & proffer themselves   like
the people of boston might trevor laid the ground-
work for the night's running joke   ice ruining
a blissful feeling that simply could have been
unlike frayed paralysis never the mcdonalds logic
of contemporary insurance micko thinks you
can protect your family from a sit-com death or
waxen misunderstandings turned bad he's not
cultured but speaks of it sanely   in a swell
psych-experiment you're a younger friend an
initiate verging on the acolytic   if you'll underline
my content riddled thought with heath ledger-esque
delivery once   more the moon might spit chunks
the candelabra might appear   outdated we're
destined to repeat our boredoms the result statistically
significant if you like (from behind those glasses

Derek Motion

Port Jackson Greaseproof Rose

Which spawned more civilisations,
yellow grass or green?

Who made poverty legal?
Who made poverty at all?

Eating a cold pork sandwich
out of greaseproof paper
as I cross to Circular Quay
where the world-ships landed poverty
on the last human continent
where it had not been known.

Linked men straddling their chains
being laughed at by naked people.

This belongs to my midlife:
out of my then suburban city
rise towers of two main kinds,
new glass ones keyed high to catch money
and brown steeples to forgive the poor

who made poverty illegal
and were sentenced here for it.

And the first Jumbo jets descend
like mates whose names you won't recall,
going down behind the city.

This midlife white timber ferry
scatters curly Bohemian glass
one molecule thick, to float above

green dark of laws older than poverty
and I hold aloft my greaseproof rose.

Les Murray

Phantom Limb

My enemy reminds me of my father:
the smell of smoke and newsprint, and the eye

behind the lens. I cannot understand the likeness:
my father was kind,

but he, my enemy,
deceives me from his empty office;

besides, my father has been dead for fourteen years.
I haven't seen my enemy for one,

but a semblance persists. He is a length of mind
which has no end. He harvests anger

and his name is myth.
His limbs hang loose and powerless,

his reasons, features, falter into word-mist,
but still he hurts me with his snarling smile.

I dreamt of him the other night
– smoke is ash's dream of being whole –

and when I woke, the only clue
to what I'd lost, like a tingling nose before the lie,

was an itch where nothing itched before,
a phantom absence: the limb I never knew I had, excised.

David Musgrave

A Bombardier on the Bus

you squirm with not enough legroom
on a crowded 442 bus
crossing the Anzac Bridge
pass two bronze soldier sentinels

called *the conscience of Parliament*
broken nose champion prizefighter
large practical hands rest on his knees
jovial smile under a brown bush hat
Tom Uren is travelling home to Balmain

a prisoner of war under the imperial Japanese
sent to work on the Burma-Thai railway
now a tourist destination:
    Major attractions
        include the River Kwai
    3 war museums   2 war cemeteries
        and the one and only   Death Railway!

an uncle of mine died at Changi
refrained from asking *did you know him?*
remember photos of skeletal survivors
Weary Dunlop   forced marches   the disease

Anzac Day celebrating war
that's really what he fought for?
kids wear medals of great-grandfather's sacrifice

pass billboards *want longer lasting sex?*
burnt out rubble
    dodgy fire at the White Bay Hotel
abandoned Power Station sprawl
the predator (infamous hot sex blogger) *doing it*
there among the pipes   concrete and aerosol scribble
heritage-listed   asbestos contaminated   toxic war zone!

Tom Uren was witness in Japan
distant mushroom cloud   atom bomb
    dropped on Nagasaki
he protests war in Iraq and Afghanistan
    marching out the front
I hobbled along
    back in the throng

Tom Uren tells me *you stay in your seat*
until the bus stops
    you could fall

Jenni Nixon

Climbing the Nectarine Tree at Dusk

The tree is growing upward fast, greedy for light,
with the best fruit already out of reach.
She wedges one bare foot where the branches fork
then steps up higher into
the sway of boughs and trunk and self;
the young tree takes her weight.
Between the fingering leaves
yesterday's stars just meeting her sight
are cold fire fruit hurtling out and away –
no fixed object in the universe.
It could be a practice one, she thinks,
a training ground for light and dark got out of hand
with earth the kindergarten of kiss and kill
(stubbornly trying to think the pattern deeper,
filling her aproned shirt, starting back down).
She sits in the cool deep clover thinking
whatever. Looking up into December. Being rich.
Then spreads the nectarines out, splits one,
sinks in. Summer syrups down her chin.
The quietness ripens into silence then ripens back.
She tries to tell scent-taste apart.
The tongue can't,
nor the mind trying the flavour of thought,
mixing sense and image and word:
a secret smile with a faintly bitter curve?

Or being fourteen with new breasts,
whispering 'mother' then 'sin'?
Another soft bite, slurping the luscious flesh.
Just 'nectarine'.
That tree knows what it's doing.
And there's Sirius out now. Seeming to hold steady.

Jan Owen

Richard Rorty
(1931–2007)

How to mourn philosophers
and not use abstract nouns?
Down here it seems that death,
your only absolute,
takes five months longer to arrive.
I see your name and then the brackets,
tight with those two dates above.
I check the internet and find
you were a 'birder' all your life,
a Trotskyite when young.
I heard you once in '99
and waited quietly in the queue
to say my shy half-dozen words.
You always sent me back to Blake:
'He who shall teach the Child to Doubt
The rotting Grave shall ne'er get out.'
I showed your ironies (boiled down)
to students in their later teens
and still can hear with pleasure
the tumble of their talk,
the need they had to 'sort things out',
to see how you had sawn away
the limbs on which their parents perched.
You taught both me and them, I hope,
how one might live with doubt,
how 'truth' deserves no capital
and won't be handed down to Moses.
You talked of better ways of talking,
of solidarity despite
the chasm under every life.

The accident of all convictions
does not, you thought, destroy
the value of a public meeting.
You spoke of what can be relinquished,
those 'chestnuts' that are best forgotten:
the holy sequence – Plato/Kant.
Learn them and forget.
You showed us how a public life
need not be commensurate
with what is in the heart,
how 'birding' won't quite change the world,
how all those Big Old Narratives
from Jesus down to Marx
should not require the self's surrender,
how such a price is way too high.
You much preferred that small 't' truth
in William James's phrase:
'What would be better
for us to believe?'
Equally, you were impressed
at how equations lift a Boeing
cleanly from the tar
which, deep deep down, has no foundation.
We soar off in its seats, content,
trying not to be obsessive.
The planets now no longer follow
Ptolemy's instructions.
Was Blake a worry to us both,
us teachers of the 'right to doubt'?
We know, of course, there's no such right.
To get it and to keep it, we
must somehow keep on talking
despite the seeming certitudes
of science – and also death.

These lines so far are what I felt,
when hearing, five months on,
that you had died in Palo Alto.
I know it's fatuous, of course,
for pragmatists to talk like this.
Too old to have a room of students,
I turn back through your essays now
(those cloudy nouns
philosophy can't do without)
hearing in the silenced print
a calm, ironic smile.

Geoff Page

'Mo' McCackie 1892–1953

A Proboscis monkey has got a nose
that hangs down 7 inches below its mouth.
The word *facetious* has got all its vowels in the right place.
A dugong is a cross between an elephant and a pig.
Chyacking: a corruption of the word *Cheek*.
'How True.   How very very True'; bouncing around
in the back of a ute (a deserted track)
apostrophizing an oath: *'You filthy
(   ) Beast! I'm a wake up to you.'   'Cop that,
young Harry!'* (Kelp is brown).
The greatest number of plates that can be
spun simultaneously is 89. People who chew (a) lot (of ice)
have got a very very very high sex drive.
In Bulgaria a nod means No, and the shaking of
the head Yes; (i'm using the crimsonest
of adjectives here) (Shooting gorillas, and dressing them up
as Clowns). *'Strike me lucky!'*
A crow's nest made up of barbwire.
'What's əəəəəəə- that?'   'A drongo!' (Cocks
are the ensigns of the Goths) (Talking about, talking about
talking (behind somebody's back)). To accost someone
is to barge straight up to 'em. Polar bear! Polar bear!
A Polar bear is left-handed; Clear the air!
A *@! fart's a combination of gasses: Nitrogen,
Nitrogen (Oxygen) Hydrogen (Sulphide).
A leer can get you a laugh on the screen. A rising
eyebrow, a Puckapunyal cocktail, a liquid
spit*ing-splu#tter (from the Palestinian parrot on a Jerusalem
    jeep);
'I got the bastards didn't i, Pal?'

It's been estimated that 80% of the animals (on
this planet) have got 6 legs. *'Other mugs
jus' haven't got it, Aye?'*
Freud identified 4 types of Humour: Hostile,
Cynical, Sophisticated, and Obscene.
A *Nip*: a ¼ of a bottle (here). (A *Baby*: an 8th or so).
Toilet paper's got a one hundred (and 40) (7) year old history.
White face.   Battered hat.   Black beard.
The inner ear))) vibrates, to let the brain know that
the head has stopped moving. (To bite
one's thumb at one!) *'That'll do, young Harry!'*
Proso'p-o-agghnosia is the complete inability to recognise
a familiar face. *'Turn up your radios, Possums!'*
The Mona Lisa's only got One eyebrow.
I don't know whether to ki*ss him, or ✓ kick him
)))))) *'Where are ya, Dad?!'*
'Gor-blimey!' You've been listening to
another episode of *McCackie's Mansion* [applause]
staring Roy Rene [applause] as 'Mo' McCackie [more]
from the sound studios of 2GB
13 Coffin Street
            Fawlty ⚡ Towers

'Oh, you dirty Mug!'

π.O.

{160}

Venery

Whoso list to hunt, I know where is an hind.—THOMAS WYATT

You slip away. I raise my crop and fly
the moon-boned strait, this sudden gate and sweat-
flanked crest; this stretch of disappointed sky.
Suspended in your absence, blooded, hooked,
my ankles' clank disturbs the night's slow pulse.
You love me, more, perhaps, than I love you,
and yet you take the deer's part every time,
leaving me these boots, this gun, my jealous chafing
thighs, my trying not to give the game away, but then
this small boxed heart I brought you here tonight
is fresh and iced, and makes me think of days
when I wore fox-fur, smiled my shot-glass smile

and lord! I had no time for men like you,
of whom, I find, there is a dearth, alas.

Felicity Plunkett

Travel

Waiting on a reeking strange
   railway station –
then the dead-quiet but crowded
   night ferry.

What country
   did I travel from
when I was born?

What alluring bait
   made me leave?

William Blake
   as he was dying
craned forward
   towards a country
he'd always wanted to see.

His rapturous curiosity
   always
      an unsettling inspiration.

The Venerable Bede
     embroidered his metaphor
       of the brevity of life
after watching
     a sparrow fly
        from one darkness to another
      a living flash
through a torch-bright hall.

What lives
    keep leaping
        to and fro
those pregnant black tunnels
        of being?

On a bold day
    my own footloose
        soul
can smell a good
        sailing wind –
the dare
    in Blake's shimmying-up-the-mast
last breath –
and then crawl
  snug and wide-eyed
  into the downy
  undercarriage
of Bede's plucky
    traveller bird.

Dorothy Porter

After Schiller

Where was I and what then happened to me
When half-light moved beyond eclipse?
Didn't I foresee the end, and you agree
Love is the clumsiest of partnerships?

And would you wish to hear me speak to you
Of irretrievable darkness by the sea;
Of happiness too far off to travel to
And in some narrow space a leafless tree?

The sound of speech, the voice of sense on earth,
In this adjunct seems carpentered of years.
My richness now is nothing but a dearth
Of tricks for the wiping-away of tears.

Moving further, may I find again
The nub of things we shared – the bridal face
Whose hurt if mine was not mine to explain
But made to seem a human commonplace?

With looking upwards hardly in my power
And being forced to seek the stars on earth,
In this exacting planisphere I cower:
I have not moved one footstep from my birth.

Weightless in everlasting space, but true
To the blindly heavy rules of time,
I have become a harbinger for you
Of every weighted station of your climb.

Peter Porter

Kate Dancing

Kate comes dancing down the stairs, her shoes
in hand, her hair swirling like a skirt.
Hair fine as a web and just as
entrancing. The spider spins by night
unwinding out of itself, wrapping
its flying moments in silken thread
to suck them dry. For sustenance, release
and the empty dawn where Kate
comes dancing, her long hair swirling
like a skirt like a silken web.
                        Night, the pallid
flicker of insect flight and the dawn we wait for
will glitter like a dewdrop. Don't, she whispers,
please don't. Restless in her sleep
she murmurs against the dark, the night
forcing an entrance where she dances
downstairs in her dreams, her shoes
clasped in her hands, her hair the web.
Outside the spider building
its silken symmetry.

                    Night
hides its surprises as drifters on their filaments
attest; and Kate, stripped of all but pain
and a bony will to dance, comes ever descending
the stairs. She does not pluck her eyebrows, now
but looks in the mirror at her thin thighs,
her restless arms. In her dreams the spider
spins as she dances downstairs. She cries
in the night like a moth, sucked dry,
androgenous, resentful. At her desk she writes
such nightmares entitled *spider web*, or
descending (ever dancing) *the stairs*.
                    Omnipotent
she seems as she writes but cannot find an end
to her flight; and the spider
who spins every night – he loves her (his silken moth)
where she comes, ever dancing, the stairs.

Ron Pretty

Morbid Transfers

i.m. Bruce Beaver

Yes, stalwart, you were right, intoning it
in that honest old-fashioned undemonstrative voice
recorded back in the Seventies. Round death
there is an eerie unremitting babble,
as with the third of your 'morbid transfers'.
No quiet is granted the lost proof reader
nestling on his page beyond typo or felicity
or 'death-dealing comma' – a handkerchief
his only shroud and a last pungent cigarette
burning down in the ashtray. Burning down.
His sole requiem is the chatter of the living,
their grim polyphony and purposing.
Not to mention the poet's sudden rapt knowledge:
'not a minute's silence will the rest of us get.'
Even seeking it, beseeching it, would be a farce.
They will babble on till the siren lures them
to their bars or chapels, their Masses or beats –
while the proof reader's mother, in her nineties,
rung up in the middle of the night, only thinks
to ask for his keys back. It comes down to this,
the domestic returns.
                        I watched it once:
death that is. *My* victim was a stranger,
a volley of raps in a void. One night
several of us were playing table tennis
in the old Olympic stadium by the lake,
puffing in our corporate T-shirts,
sweat forming new industrious logos.

The gym was packed with duos and foursomes,
all graded as in life or commerce,
the waspish ones capable of spin
infinitely closer to the door and glory –
a kinetic conference like a dream of Bosch.
Low fences separated the courts,
low fences to stop balls and sequester
the gods from the inglorious,
the spinners from those of us incapable of slant.
Looking round mid-point, disturbed by something
(instinct or a second's spastic silence),
I saw the brilliant boy already prostrate where he served,
so quick no one had registered the fall,
not even his opponents, eyes only on the ball.
Soon they gathered round him, incredulous,
almost jovial at first, thinking it a prank,
then urgent and clamorous and shrilly capable,
ripping at the shirt with its own bleached logo,
then standing back to marvel at the scar
stitching down his chest,
though he was only eighteen or twenty
or whatever they are when it happens –
whatever it is. Then someone, surer,
with a certificate, was pumping the boy,
rhythmic as a metronome, pausing now and then
to measure the effect as if with dough.
Nil, the minutes told us. Nil effect.
                         Others came,
rows of them: a punctilious chemist,
an off-duty policeman who was playing nearby,
then authorities and paramedics
and the weary manager of the stadium,
almost querulous at this cessation
so late in the night, just ten minutes to go.

By now so many things were obvious
the four of us put away our silly bats and balls,
half ashamed – half ashamed to be leaving alive.
Elsewhere the games, those few interrupted,
began to resume, tentative at first then louder,
with a new kind of wilfulness and artistry,
as if making up for lost time –
so that despite the blatant cardiac affront
all we could hear was the gossip of balls
and the futility of widening scores
and the sibilance of rubber soles
as they slid and slid and slid –
until it was a kind of mutiny,
'the loud chanting of the living',
their way of saying to the irresponsive boy
this was their angle, their tactic, their victory,
a kind of spin that none of us enjoyed.
Finally, a bouncing ball invaded the mortuary
and the server, too spirited for niceties
or condolences, stepped over the low excluding fence,
negotiated the crumpled mystery at his feet
and retrieved his urgent ball without a word.

Peter Rose

In the fifth of Bruce Beaver's *Letters to Live Poets* (1969), Bruce Beaver writes about 'three images of dying'. The third death takes place in a newspaper office, where the dead proof reader is abandoned at his desk. Beaver recorded the poem in the 1970s. Three marked phrases, including the title, are taken from Beaver's poem.

Is the light right?

If only everything were as simple
as the back road home:
dark sage sea with its crushed ice fringe
under that sudden cheek of cloud in a coral sky,
a single wind turbine above the dunes
spinning its spiky limbs into power
without fusion or dust,
Charles Wright on the tape deck
tonguing language into a white water,
raising bones from the dead
talking with ghosts,
and the spirit of poetry
rising in me like a prayer.

If only, when the moon floats up like that,
a green shimmer as if it stole the sea's gauze veil
dragging it up higher and higher,
then dropping it to flush its watermelon glaze in the sunset,
the earth didn't turn in for the night,
turn away, turn its back,
but rose toward the dark smiling.
What if tomorrow, light is too big when it comes,
never a shadow to rest in,
no blood-warming pools of dark water to drink from,
sky never again boot-black and anxious,
and I forever driving through burning day
along ten thousand miles of loneliness.

Robyn Rowland

Tormented Syllogism Held at Bay

Each day you remember an entire life
festooned with silence, enthralled by a tree
and walk back into the legend of the beach's
zipped water and bucking dolphins
Another predecessor's dug up
a cheese-grater in its heyday
another meteor shower
Plastic sacks hang like scales
and websites tick into the ether
polling your consumption or pity

The interrupted CD's broken aerial
makes you try surprise
old Maroochydore of the mind
bumped up with the available
as when the cherried sky falls behind the dishes
jutting a wagging finger
a wind-up statuette of pure intention
perfecting the art of the suburbs
through the pale supermarket's aisles

Or drive into the intersection's law that no one follows
out of one life into another
automatic roads and washed rhododendron
wails the redemption song
whose 'hearts are out of order'
that Pyramis and Thisbe scat
Crayon elm and stitched grass sink for you,
and planes open the canned estates
printed on a ridge

She folds her hard-earned into a platypus
– a market for your thoughts – and reassures his elbow
A proscenium of other lives ascends into the heavens
Bright star I wish I were as remote and singular
sparkling in the debris and not a mash
Ships slip the horizon
and unharmed novelists walk home in leaking sun
She dusts herself off and keels over in a binge
She was the ones she loved
Farewell youthful carousers most unwritten
Remember sea beneath the gulls, now clouds nod in the
 buildings
and Goth Estate Agents twirl the rivet keys

Gig Ryan

Reading Francis Webb

Tiled rooves in Orange miraging around you, the nerving
home above the park, the mad and ordinary moments
washed by the common soap. From this battered linoleum

ordinary you founded intensity and God. The poems
rhymed into the past with grace and violence, your pure impure
directions, your long wires, your inner Spinning Jenny.

Inside the pyjamas, the drugs, the chance, a teleology
was rolling through the '50s television screen, its vertical hold
there and nowhere as you sat around chomping apples,

the ones you didn't drop, alone in that rising gravity
you heard equally in Jussi Björling or in the mad-for-God
supplicants you saw wandering your imagination, or eating

from refectory plates on Sunday evenings, or smudging
through letters to the godofnoaddress by the poor unfamilied
schizophrenics. The after-life for itinerants.

The fruit-pickers have come to pick and the garden's
full of secateurs, like sanity, so sharp you shrink back into poetry,
or should those clarities be reversed?

God's the trick. Not the skin, the blight, the dapple and myrrh,
the impure pure and cortex-firing ecstasies we might *call* God
but the dogma of God. Like Beaver, the under-terror. All.

The black hole. The rifling of chalices, Eucharists, the closed
text pretending it is open. Your own, thankfully, the open
text hoping it was closed. You let God in. You let us in.

Philip Salom

The Pain Switch

The moon's white knife, etching its cold
signature in your skin, strikes bone.
Butoh shapes snap across the ruin
of your face, taut as a top sheet in a ward.
The pain switch is useless, morphine enough
to kill a horse bucked off. As am I,
awake at the foot of your bed, listening
to your c fibres fire, packets of fascist
electrochemical mail stitching up
your body's free speech each split second.
I've become devout, pray each time
the coming dark snags in your throat.
Sunlight smirks through the curtain
when the nurse shakes my wrist,
saying *It's time*. I grasp your hand,
realise you've been holding on for this:
your vanquished sigh, a sharp, hot fist.

Jaya Savige

Necromantic

for Martin Harrison

André Gide, once dead, becomes reanimated
a century past, re-pens *Les Nourritures Terrestres*
whilst drinking cognac on Darlinghurst Road.

He works through spring and into summer
without shifting tables, shadows swallowing
every stroke in heat and traffic

the endless Sanskrit flow of his hand.
His lips a half-pout wet with drink and think
ing and everywhere the air thinned

of memories, smells, of the revenants
competing for noise on this corner, this
small slice of presence

their purgatory: you see
it's not the filament touch of it – the fine threads
connecting the bulbous sheen of cognac

to windshields, sunglasses, the passing sirens,
brightness, another afternoon announcing God
in a clash of brass percussion

and certainly not our bodies
which break and fade and eat themselves
even as we watch

not cymbals – but words, that
he wants the light to be permanent
which is the only game in town. And yes

Mont St-Michel is a mirage on a tide
cracked earthen spires on blue tidal sheen
but then so is Victoria Street, and Liverpool

all the city's vibrant squalor. So he sits
at Le Petit Crème, writing light into time
in the ebb and flow of traffic, and the city's

arc of sun
writing itself in cracks of pavement,
the translucent lines of his skin.

Berndt Sellheim

Monteverdi at 74

1.
I have seen too much.
The politics of power,
The access to greed
Even in the supposed humble.
Nero is never a stranger
He is one of us.

2.
I do not have to look far
To see corruption.
Corruption is not a word
To be used about strangers.
It is in our blood,
And the longer we have
The more it resembles
That other word: hypocrisy.

3.
I, too, was once young.
I was in love
And my wife died
Too soon after marriage.
Feeling is all we have
To cling on to.
Strange that feeling
Can be the force
Behind corruption,
The guiding power
Within hypocrisy.

4.
Without feeling
We are automatons
And there are many
Who have perfected the art,
Which they call 'disinterest'
(not to be confused
with the lack of same).
But feeling will not be denied
Even though it adopts
Perhaps strange forms.

5.
Love is a strange form.
For me it was a salvation,
A guiding light
Through the labyrinth
Of youth and the insatiable body.
Interesting that in old age
Such feeling remains.
It is perhaps a wonder
Even though all the elements
Will conspire against us.

6.
Corruption is not so much
An absence of restraint
As a surplus of feeling's insatiability.
Had my wife lived
I might have found other forms
To translate this surplus of feeling.
I might have corrupted
Myself and others.

As it was, I descended to song
As if that might relieve me
Of grief, of tension.
By finding a cadence for feeling
I held time at bay; yes, that is true.
But I also courted pretence –
I could tell that in every listener
Who became moved by my music.
No, it was not hypocrisy
It perhaps flirted with corruption
But it truly expressed me,
Or the me I needed others
To respond to.

7.
Hence Nero and Poppea.
Do not be fooled
By the wisdom of Seneca.
I am the nurse who rubs hands
At the immediate power.
Nothing lasts
But feeling is not about that.
Welcome to my new opera.
We are all in it,
Every one of us.
You will be strangely moved
By the power of corruption.
Is this all we, finally, have?

Thomas Shapcott

Slipper

Slip your feet in the shoes of the water,
the fake-leather brown of it, and wear standing.
Your pair of red bunch of toes – eel-boots in river – so current-long
the ends of them turn up like fashion.
Pebble and pop of caverns letting their fluid out where banks burst.

Sea is miles away walking in its own pair of tides.
Here you can break in a horse of white water
and not be spilled where you trap it in your thighs,
it is froth-lame with rocks.
Name it Curry for its shandy-dirty sands.
Bareback it till your hands can fin no more, so cold and numb.
Then, leg after leg, you mortar and pestle back home over crunch,
though home is gone. Look all you like for someone there
they are loving in other places with another you.
Night lisps and warns in the pines.

Craig Sherborne

Lives

Of an evening he'd be haunting the scriptorium
    in research after Plutarch or Livy;
for in truth he was a quite tireless scholar,
    should the passion happen to assail him.

    When she trapped him strolling the corridor,
entangled in a volume of the *History*,
    she permitted her demurest gesture
to alight upon the precipice of a smile,

and then brushing at his elbow she succeeded
    in one eyebrow tilting suggestively.
He appeared never to have noticed, or
    if noticing declined to acknowledge it,

    yet she knew as her footfall diminished
that he'd halted there and made no further progress.
    Was he stumped by a difficult passage
as he headed for the shelter of his library;

startled by some clause that he'd recycle
    in Latin at the table over breakfast?
Or had her little ornament winged him,
    releasing sudden worlds and possibilities?

    The others were inclined to dismiss him with a
blend of admiration and irony,
    but she believed she'd glimpsed through to some quality
beyond the thin delvings of the learned;

she was curious, and determined more than ever
    to unhitch his curtains of contentment,
his apparent undistractible devotion
    to those musty yellow tomes he lived in.

    And she found herself not quite unready,
in the Romanesque refectory next morning,
    when his glances from across the toast-rack
seemed to hazard an appeal of recognition –

but as well, in a most delicate manner,
    a requestioning of her deeper intention.
As they left he fumbled his tractatus,
    touched her elbow with such classical restraint.

Alex Skovron

Triptych

Lethal injection is delivered in three stages, with a
saline solution in between substances to clear the line.

I. Sodium thiopental (5 grams)

Fastened to the board, a tube grips
the wall of your final vein. Fresh pants
and shirt, the spoor of shampooed hair.
A pulse recurrent as a tidewheel.

> *A wave courses up the beach, rinses*
> *what junks the tide has thrown up,*
> *then furls up to dissolve in the sea.*

II. Pancuronium bromide (100 mg)

Only the fated know when there are
only minutes left. Tied to a plank
at sea, rising over troughs of swell,
the land disappears with each drop.

> *A wave courses up the beach, rinses*
> *what junks the tide has thrown up,*
> *then furls up to dissolve in the sea.*

III. Potassium chloride (100 mg)

By now you wouldn't even feel
the baitfish nibbling at your ankle;
the squid slipping its hand out of
yours, as if leading you out to dance, out to sea.

Andrew Slattery

In the Butterfly House, Vienna

I expected silk and colour, old brocade,
exotic palpitations, streaks of gold,
rosenkavaliers flirting in the shade,
but suddenly the day turned cold.

Was this the wrong time, or the wrong year,
a switch forgotten yesterday?
A few were starting to cause fear,
cloth that flutters as it rots away,

and several had an eye patch on each wing,
drawing to repel admiration,
staring one way, flying off the other

wanting to be thought some other thing.
One tried an occasional gyration –
call it a final fling, brother.

Vivian Smith

This Machine Kills Fascists

I.

Bob Dylan wrote this on his guitar
He was in Gaslight Café wearing Woody Guthrie's underwear
ready to play his new songs. What people didn't know was
that Bob Dylan wasn't real. He was a pastiche of shaken
experimental noise, a meta-wobble of fuzzy pitch, a pert peach
& a salty A string. His guitar was a chaos weapon, ready to
destroy liars. Dylan was put on this earth to fizzle the critics &
squash the hinges off blind believers.

Dylan loved to snitch out the liars by playing
recordings of different brands of guitar &
getting them to guess which one it was:
the muffle of the candy apple red Jazzmaster, the molten
twang of the tobacco sunburst '62 (complete with pickguard
swirls), the disposable sound of the mid-'50s Kay Silverstone,
the puffed strings of a '60s Gibson acoustic.
The deluxe cocktail of all four.
If the listeners misjudged the origin of the sound they were
never heard from again. He would pluck that vibrating A string
& the universe would have its way.

II.

I think of a hero as someone who understands the degree of responsibility that comes with his freedom. — BOB DYLAN

He stood there at Gaslight with the knowledge
that guitars are ambassadors to the soul.
The patchwork of sounds blending with the fabric
of skin. The lavish lust of melody. The show of rhythm. The
whack of minimum perfection. He felt these aural pleasures on
the flap of his old suit pants and thought: all music is its own
biological system. Everything needs connection. The string
& the bass. The lips & the tongue. The hole & the jack. The
hormones & receptors. Parasites & hosts. *Sticky sex* he called it.
He wanted to solve all he could with the sass of a Stratocaster
& the grit of guitar gristle.

This is where he transformed into a psychotronic wave of
language & light & marked this century. Where he was in
harmonious frequency with the star system
he came from. He stood in Hopper light & peered through
his kaleidoscope. He took a big breath. He was ready to be
famous, ready to be human. Blissfully unaware of what this
would mean: the scratch fights, the hisses, long nights of
drink & gods, the loveless thanks. He pulled his happy trigger
of strings & melted quickly into the form of a man. No one
noticed. He only impaled a few fakes that night.

He was introduced & shook a little with the coffee crowd.
Only small memories of his home remained. He looked
down at his guitar, saw the writing & wanted to share the
experience. He walked up to the microphone to say something
but thought better of it. He's been doing this for nearly fifty
years. Only sometimes
when he mumbles, those close can hear:
stand back
this guitar's got a lotta kick.

Alicia Sometimes

Anaesthetic

for David McCooey

    Valium-nice, this business of death,
this chemical smile
    that floats my body, bundled in snow and hay,
above a hospital tray,
    where flesh and time take wing like sin,
and I become
    this white light and space,
pure, nothing.

    Is this what they waited for,
those god-heavy trolls,
    with their big hands and brown eyes,
as they crouched
    with their mercury liquor under dank stone bridges,
year after year,
    in summer grass and winter sludge, until they
drowned themselves there:

    my great uncle, whose leg was shot off among
the mottled birch
    where Soviet tanks and silent Finnish gunmen played at chess
in the snow;
    my youngest uncle, who stole from his old mother to slake
his darkling thirst;
    and my eldest cousin, who died only months ago, leaving
a drunk ex-wife and a son with myopia?

    Is this what I wanted during those leaden times,
when with every mouthful
    I swallowed the burning world, offering myself to
the execution and release
    of an earth-bound history, and is it
what I am given now
    only because I am godless (except for you)
and happy?

    Meanwhile, Egyptian morticians manage my corpse
for resurrection.
    I wake to the human condition
– mine anyway –
    heavy as a hangover, but faithful to the miracles
of science,
    so much kinder than religion, and to your imminent
and hallowed coming.

Maria Takolander

Cimitière Marin Revisited

Sète, Summer 2008

The building by the gate declares
Easy Sushi Made in 7.
Must be most of Valéry's fans are Yanks
or from Sydney. Those from Europe
or Melbourne would prefer their food slow
and local. After the climb
from the port more than the sky-blue soul
needs sustenance.

Easy Sushi Made in 7,
each grain of rice shining like a tomb
or an individual gull, harsh, blank
against the sea. The nori rolls
wrapped in seaweed dark as cypress
ooze soy sauce the way
a coffin in a cheap horror movie
might exude something ill-defined.

Sashimi glints like the flecks of sun
on the Mediterranean, a stripper's
sequins, carved marble, a tourist's lens.
Easy Sushi Made in 7
raises the question: Why not five?
Is it just for the obvious rhyme
the lazy translator will make
with *ciel*? Or is precision all?

Valéry called the sea a faithful sheepdog bitch
lying across the foot of this final bed,
keeping at bay those *banzai* idolators
who would storm the heights with similes
as sharp as wasabi.
Today they come by plane to taste
Easy Sushi Made in 7.
It's OK. They don't do lamb.

Food that melts into joy in the mouth
was a metaphor for the rapture
of the poet's future: soul meunière?
But a bad pun is as a dodgy prawn
down at a canalside café or up here at
Easy Sushi Made in 7
where the indifferent sky
makes bitterness sweet and clears the mind.

I think about dead strangers.
Their photos and flowers, their
brief, carved bios cannot re-flesh
the bones below. Life, like
Easy Sushi Made in 7,
is too quick. And the dead
are too long subjects for meditation.
Their oblivion outlasts art.

Immortality is the beautiful lie,
or so said Valéry. I'm not so sure
about its beauty, nor about its falsehood.
Sleight like the chef's or like the ad man's
Easy Sushi Made in 7
can con its way into eternity.
Sincerity's the key. Whatever you write
or cook should seem sincere,

then you might have a chance at ugliness
that lasts forever. Up here
the air, at least, is freshly caught,
while we can overlook for now
what the daikon pushes through,
gathering health, before it makes it
as far as the bench where it is sliced for
Easy Sushi Made in 7.

The view from this roof to
the fish wharf's smell, above
the crowds who buy and sell along
the Rue Paul Valéry, is still splendid.
The fishermen lost, down with the tuna,
their bones rattling like chopsticks in
Easy Sushi Made in 7,
have their blue blanket rolled out by the tides.

The tombstones are still cooing, poised
like carrier pigeons, each with its message:
'Eat. Drink. *Memento mori.*'
Consume and die, whether it's
Easy Sushi Made in 7
or the surface of the sea
flat as a Sanyo plasma screen
and bluer, too. Who would rather

Zeno's arrow than a dove
or gull? Fluency even while
dipping or chopping gives the illusion
of speed, and this is what we get from
Easy Sushi Made in 7,
forgetting the long build-up,
discounting the time it takes
for salt to crystallise.

Easy Sushi Made in 7:
the claim confronts. Check your watch.
The Valéry Museum closes for lunch,
for longer even than seven minutes
plus walking time along the paths
that flank white oblongs of stone
as ropes edge sails. Fit attendants
can digest at leisure, even read.

And what would they read? What would
any of us read, here under the shade
of a cypress, perched on the edge
of some family's petrified grief?
What verses help digest
Easy Sushi Made in 7?
Whatever is chosen, remember
the wind that slammed Paul's book shut.

'The sea's breath,' he called it
as it snuffed out poetry
and hurled him back to life,
inspired. Is it too far-fetched
to imagine him as a short-order cook,
slinging noodles at
Easy Sushi Made in 7,
feeding his own pilgrims?

He's here, at least. I have climbed
to find him, not expecting
Easy Sushi Made in 7
as a bonus, but being sure
that the cemetery would provide
a feast, not just for worms, bacteria,
but to satisfy the hunger growing
since first I read 'Le Cimitière Marin'.

Tim Thorne

The Light Went Off in Me

The light went off in me.
The light went off
And in that stillness
The dying walked from me.

Abandoned ship, the sails that
Puckered my fingers into lanterns.
The light dried up.
The sun was carried off on a fish.

Its neon skull loved nothing,
Crawled from my bones, left *all* gaping.
I stood over a body with the light
Off in me, with the sky behind my fingers

While I withered into the pale flute
Of the light that went off in me.
To get back my light
I let my heart be bent, easily as steel,

My bones be dipped into gold.
But the light did not return.
It did not want me back so I
Ate the light and it sat in me

Like a lantern, dimmed in the wind
That howled through me, left a trail of
Smoke and ash, a rustic core,
Forever barren of seed.

Jessika Tong

The Anaglyph

Hasn't the charisma leaked away from the café crowd, and that other
Authority, the *Salon des Refusés*? I have forgotten much of
That old sack of enthusiasms and snake-oil recipes, the way
You have forgotten your own childhood, since
You woke up just in time to watch the adults disappear
From the world they had bequeathed us. It seems the scenery all around
Is hilly and unfarmable. Being brilliant has been reckoned
Into a procedure by some old guy, with a motto that is
More fitness, less flab. I hanker to go back to the land.
This means ruin to the culture-watchers. But the basic
Principle of my ambition is to be one excessively distracted
Entity at the mercy of the lurid, blurred and half-perceived
Motions of the Martians at the Halloween Hop. Fake? They sure are.
Summer is called Humidor here, the month of damp draughts.
The tale of my attempt to farm stubborn soil leaked from
Untruth to legend, my unlikely phase of boy-scout honesty being
Before I came to the big city. Here behind the tiny horological waterfall
Drums amplify the fun, but only at nightfall, then just for a moment
Of horrible error as I clutch the wrong person's hand. That was true,
Only I said it wrong. Ugh. Now watch my serpentine
Gesture as I withdraw my hand, only to replace it with a congruent
Message that attempts to excuse this tactless fact,
Tearing at the sky over Twenty-second Street, but
The sky leans nonchalantly against the coop – I mean 'co-op' – about

As graceful as a cowboy leaning on a chicken co-op – I mean
    'coop' – who either
Has an anger management problem or is under the influence
    of a form of
Some anxiety that eats at him. I'm not the fly-away
Marrying kind, nor a grumpy bachelor with a broken heart
    whose pieces
Are seen scattered over the range. That begs for an independent
Yet symbolic judgment from the Judge now alighting from the
    caboose, whose arrival
Whether timely, to the tick of a caesium atom, or tardy, has to be
Seen to be believed, like
The face of a hunter in the dim mirror killing a bear. As
Nostrils give away suppressed anger by flaring, so an argument
That is over leaves traces – nervous twitch, grimace. It
Is impossible to hide my feelings, I guess. Look ahead,
That effervescent persona and its emotional lurches and
    rocketings
Affected so much, and its magnum opus that was called
By another name is now the old schoolteacher's chief act of belief,
Or something very like it, gleaming in the rain. Hold up that light.
Has it shone on the tenebrous backyards yet? Or yet admitted that
It is unable to illuminate the wasteland of wet barbecues, so much
Of its fuel has flared and lit up the landscape … this project, I
    admit that
It is like gutting then refurbishing a friend's apartment. Now, are
The reply and the echo finished with? I asked a redundant
    question, and
That answer suffocated it, as a firmly pressed pillow
Has choked a banker, but no one knows whodunnit. That whole
    thing
Of returning to my sources, raking through my prototypes until
The last blueprint is found and seems just right: perhaps this is
Peace – a crowded peace – under the hot sun.

That we are afraid of it – inhabiting a reputation, the whole thing
About establishing who you genuinely were – are – I'll admit. There
You hope your opus will be taken for legerdemain, but your effort sinks
Deeper into the mulch of history, while I adjust the mask that
Just fits more loosely every decade, and then I add up the little
That memory leaves me, a kind of pittance, the totality
Mustered and gathered ... a look of boredom in a young person's eyes,
And all those hopes and struggles are quite lost.
Accents and dialects distort them, once again.
To have escaped from a tangle of difficulties, from
Nothing but obstructions, into a glowing absence
And then to take a deep breath and plunge into
Those crowded riverine cities, greedy for contact with ghosts that are
Precisely what we want them to be, our plans furthered,
Seeing alphabet soup spell out the aleatory message and the time,
Casting caution to the winds and the weather – sorry, welter
Of neighbours, barking dogs, traffic cops – it leads to a general confusion.
And permit me ... no, commit me, please, while the cops are standing
Around chewing the fat, and pray that these
Moments miss you like a whistling arrow. Thunk! The old tapir tapered
Into the bar: a Scotsman, an Irishman and a capybara – I've heard it. But
Wasn't the story of an Eskimo inside an eviscerated bear like this?
The fact that he 'inhabited' the smelly bear-skin ... I feel that
Neither brave feats nor stories about them can cut it.

Did not a Dandy Dinmont yap? I deliberately stayed
This way, spiritually a hunchback, drooling and gaping at the stars
That promised ashes and diamonds and nourishing food all the way,
As though clambering inside an animal was simply the reverse
Of some method of becoming notorious. My cheating heart is known
Once its modus operandi is – among the cognoscenti – firmly established.
The look of a man is the man, Buffon said, and style a condition
Of those whose reputation is a handbag and whose blindness
Was being talked about even in Paris: a troubling myopia, so
That their left and right perceptual fields, red and green, slowly separated,
Only to hitch up again, like inspiration and perspiration. Go on, shout
And be heard. Is this anaglyph what I really want? My declamatory
Nature was made to seem just a yokel act. I must admit it is
Not without a certain eau-de-cologne charm, insinuated the farmer. And yet
An invisible horror prevents me from making love to you among the previsions,
Then the post-visions I am subject to arrive, fits of
The assurance Baron Corvo had an excess of, a crowing assurance
Which tainted his career, under the blasts of air conditioning,
Whatever. There on the bank statement
At the beginning of the Age of Façadism was a catalogue of waste.
A dumb waiter brought me the tablets and a note about the projected
After-effects, should they amplify the symptoms instead of curing them,

Though Frederick Rolfe was never cured. This
Emptiness will do fine. Just pop it in a doggy bag, thanks. Did
 you say 'previsions'?
Was that a mispronunciation? 'Provisions', maybe, held
Too close to the chest, a fake poker hand of fate. The fireworks,
 they
Ended with a fizzing Roman candle sound that frightened the
 guest who was
Intended to rescue Gertie McDowell from that dirty old man. It's
Gesture that fills out the role, as water makes the weather.
It was stupid of me to harp on the sadness
Of that animal's demise: I should forget about the feeling
Which resembles taxidermy at midnight on an empty highway.
A telescope brings us a soothing view of distant mountains
And all the mountain people. Who knows where they're going?
Moving from crag to cave to avoid the night
There, which is really ghastly when it comes on.
Beside the darkness, each farmer carries his own personal
Landscape around inside his head, a 'landscape' being
What surrounds your idea of yourself, it's so
Honourably framed, but presented in a Potemkin-Village spirit.
There was a vast electrical disturbance just outside the walls.
Each time it's different, down through the centuries
For the sake of cultural improvements they go on repeating a
 dream that
Continually gives out a soft fluorescent glow, it was
Like standing on the prow of a moving ferry in the morning
With the spray bursting all around
And a feeling of nausea mixed with ecstasy washing over me.
 In a way
The whole experience was fake, except for the scale.
Really, what do Eskimos think of giants?
Not too much, I reckon. They say they like them.
A moment later they're saying how needlessly big they are. But
Also they are likely to flatter them. A cloud of dust

Or whirling fragments resembling a mistral rises up ahead,
But no one understands it: the old verbal torrent
In new guise, transformed into a sheaf of falling leaves, which
Are gathered up, bound and stuffed into a briefcase,
And it's time for coffee and a Strega at Il Miglior Fabbro. When
Acts of killing fill nightmares and movies, only the calm
Of this bibulous routine can bring surcease. Then the shreds
Of another adventure assemble: a tour through the old college
    premises
Undertaken to the tune of the jig 'From Rochester he came
    hence,
A writ of Cease and Desist clenched in his teeth'. Here, see this,
Like a pistol on a silver platter, it's all yours
And it was mine once. Take it, go on. I kept it because
It had been handed down, and I had hoped it might be my
    insurance
Against the waves of devoted fans inefficiently
Seeking to take over the social scene and then the whole world.
The round platter, alas, has always been covered with dust,
So small it can hardly hold the pearl-handled revolver reclining
    on it.
Thereafter it should be passed on to other worthies, noted by
The comfort of strangers they fail to offer you, or me, even.
Like the wily coyote, I'm no sleep-abed; I tried all
The most difficult forms, even threnodies ending with the words
'After all' or 'Never mind!' And in my fine eye-rolling frenzy I
    almost
Exaggerated my metier into an obligation. This,
It seemed, was the way to build the future. But it was
Not likely to allow me to escape the whirligig of voracious time.
After all, *tempus fugit* however we might chase it. Indeed,
All kinds of regret sprinkled my breakfast as the slant angle of
The day lit up the diner and the light began to increase
So that I was dazzled, then I heard a loud thump, dull, heavy,
Like a polar bear falling over, and the hunter saying something

Not quite obscene, but close enough. *Criminy!* The way
Things fade away, *le temps perdu* seems to be the point
Of this rodomontade. Does a traditional verse form simply
   provide
A protected place for the poet to plead the case for his vital
Concern for *la vie littéraire*, or is it a carapace, a palace?
And you can meditate there all summer long.
It was a little insight I had, one of the world's smallest.
Distant requests annoy me. The Poetry Club may be ultra-
   sensitive
But its supine and self-serving acquiescence
To the demands of those creeps … okay, that's in the past
And it belongs there and I promised not to whine. But oh, how
The past haunts me, its vapid fashions, the rigmaroles … they
   wish
But also harangue, that's why I resent them, the ones I talk with.
And in this way my paean to non-discovery
In brittle yet oracular verse persuades us, but nevertheless
The map you provided was helpful in leading us beyond
Madness to something better: squatting in Circe's mansion. Only
You desire us to fail – just there, perhaps, where your verbal acts
Are sentinels warning us of the slow-moving, quiet
Invasion of middle America by pod people over many years.
Be quiet – hush! – they are nearby, whispering the poem itself
In a parody of oratory. I'll explain more plainly: the map
Of the literary world is a pantomime, and its longeurs have
   become
Prolongations of our prevarications on bad weather days, and
   also
Fine days where things seem okay but are not, those dull events
We shall banish from the Ideal Republic. Who called? No, I am
Not speaking to that shit: he just wants to be
Opposite me at the literary lunch. He got some fame recently,
   only
To be thrust into obscurity soon, I hope. It seems broader,

The sum total, a canal reflecting its own anagram, but will it ever
Become legible? Hidden behind a screen of rocks
And foliage, the creep quickly inhales the distant
Ether and faints, thank goodness, and what I own
I see before me shining like a dagger. Meanwhile
I am only me, a faithful shadow of my real self, and
Private doubts evaporate between the Spring and the Fall
And even this is seasonal, and I thank you
For being so patient, you could have made some other
Voluntary or involuntary gesture like sneezing to prove your
Maturity or you could have hung and dangled from the branches
Of a tree to attract my attention a step or two away from them.
It intensifies my desire to know you, a gesture like that, to
Form an opinion of your feints, apparitions and mode of locomotion.
In this way I control the crowded avenue to the Palace of Fame, the one
Leading to a rowboat mounted in a park where I perch and think to
Myself and then jot it down, being careful to leave a blank space
That is the secret indication of Mallarmé's abyss, a.k.a. 'The Unknown'.
Eating ragwort is morally better than gobbling a quail tagine; the difference
Can never be explained to the obtuse. At this distance
It seemed impossible to reach the reader, Valéry murmured, then said the phrase
'Over and over' to himself, again and again. Meanwhile
Infant mortality was declining as aspirin consumption increased. There was
To be a meeting about aspirin and other drugs later that evening,
He was told. He read poems about killing large animals to keep awake

On the tepid waters of café society. Go to the meeting, don't go,
    whatever.
'Whose centre wobbles is bound to fail', the Latin motto says,
    and having
The progression of the equinox too much in mind brings rain
As they form a phalanx of epigones, those who come after.
Why don't they just get used to that? They can't be equal
Without coming before, and that's impossible. The cup of
Contentment will never touch their lips. Ministering
To stunted talents is my fate; each day I tread that lonesome
    trail alone
And return at nightfall bereft and grinding my teeth at
What they dish out: similes as appliqué aperçus. They
Might as well hand in embroidery. The Force, puissant yet
    invisible,
Still surrounds us. Yet there is also a Dark Force
Between the cruel mandates of history and them.
It is because the greatness of art is like a snobbish relative
That we shall never agree on a strategy, and
Entertainment washes over us, leaving us ethically incomplete.
Former East German border guards know too well that that
Closes off an awful lot of options. The Moment
Of Death is dallying on Ninth Avenue, as yet uncertain of
Its intentions. I'll just leaf through the paper until
You wake up. I'm not planning to go anywhere. You know, it
Wasn't a small thing, to turn your back on Europe. The walls
Are turning into their own murals. Please don't speak
Of time within the hearing of that tiny hydraulic clock you
Invented, it can be self-centred and jealous, and has now
Grown furious. Deep within its complex innards a purple jewel
Exists as a blazon, rotating slowly, saying that this
Existence is temporary, that you may lodge and idle here
Only so long as you don't irritate the gods. Someone's
Purpose niggles at you. Then the sunbeams flood in at acute
Angles and frighten the other diners. I thought, then,

Of having whatever I wanted, but it seemed that a distant
Image of you chided me. My admiration is a test
Of how you might accept it: gracefully, or boorishly, or not.
You hesitate, don't you? I hate that. Please accept this
Wooden gesture, and you're right, the over-decorated
    representation
Returns whence it came, though it was easily said, and simply
    meant,
With nothing ulterior about it: a *simple entendre*. I'd like to alight
With you from the caboose on a hot dry day in a wonderful
    town. You
Must help the Judge measure the exact length of the shadow of
Your well-wrought urn in the centre of the town square – it is
    still intact;
Appreciation gives it the shine and the shadow – but just now
    somebody
is phoning to arrange for drinks – will you join me? – later this
    evening.

John Tranter

An anaglyph is a red-green pattern providing a stereoscopic image. The first and the last word or two in each line of this poem are the same as the first and the last word or two from the corresponding line of John Ashbery's 1977 poem 'Clepsydra'. A general critical or creative piece of writing was commissioned by *The Modern Review* for a special feature on 'Clepsydra' in 2007; the choice of this form was the author's.

Improvisations on a Daylight Moon

1.
The boy hits a tennis ball with a yellow plastic racquet,
and above him the summer sky
                                      is as blue as a plexipave court.
Near the baseline on his forehand side, the moon has left a mark.
Though the boy disputes the call, the ball was well in.
                                              An out and out
winner. Love–thirty. Coming on for noon.

2.
In the stricken sky
the daylight moon is a skull
cap without a skull.

3.
If you cracked an egg
and poured out a day
like this, the half-moon
in the two-o'clock sky
is what would be left.

4.
I don't understand how, in the brightness
of the day, the moon loses the body it uses
at night and becomes a diaphanous cawl.

5.
By night the moon's your mistress
and the night is her bed;
by day she's as holy and insubstantial
as Hildegaard von Bingen.

6.
The day is a blue pasture turning grey in the heat. God hays
the morning long and rolls it tall
                                 in cloudstacks and the wind backs
to the south and then rain falls. God's got a migraine now;
                                        her vision's occluded,
her mood's turned sour. The afternoon spends everything
the morning saved. And the moon dissolves
                                        like an aspirin in a glass.

7.
What else did you see, Dad, when you were a little boy? What did you see from your cowshed when you were a little boy? I saw the moon, my boy. I still see the moon. Do you see the moon?

Mark Tredinnick

Torture is a Dirty Word

Voices from outside the cemetery

Very well then, comrade, and if our time has gone
we still have gesturing that can be made,
stuccoed upon the reef:
the merely personal whistles like a wren
or trills our nerve-ends with a few volts.

But, busy enough, sloping under a little
clump of errant bluegums here
when the day's grown aromatically warm,
that reminiscent perfume just about
rips out my heart.

Very well then, or not, an age has passed
stranding on a gritty reef all those
who rode a plank raft of ideals,
working to protect the little fish,
when there still was a secular god.

The Dirty Word

Walking under winking wattle
that burns the winter away
resist the paradoxical way
in which the viridian tide of pleasure
makes one taste of death.

But if we fail to murmur death
we cannot hear the sound of blood,
nor touch those random victims who
cry out from the very moment
when the electrodes are applied;

for torture is the dirty word
and some are trying to clean its face.
There can be nothing quite like
hypothetical fear to rouse
the deepest human nastiness.

If the cut worm has any sense
it will not forgive the plough,
but let's not hear the word, revenge:
a dragon that must feed on
all the pornography of shame.

Chris Wallace-Crabbe

Three Rivers Triptych

NIGHTJAR

he lifts his hands and wipes fat brushes over shiny clusters
attentive to sound (as an image) the owl's nocturnal call
figures in his thoughts
as he fastens his gaze and paints (something akin to)
a night bird's song

night becomes apparent in the colours that night allows
a sky has its satellites its shooting stars
falling in his hands and shining eyes
onto canvas

    *

HIS SON'S CHAIR

(for the two dieters)

in the wilderness where he wakes he also sleeps
working paints onto a canvas as wide as night
sharp as the stretched colours that peak so vivid

                      (and should the painting ask
can you hear that?) you could say
that the eye frames the sound of an ocean at your feet
the sound of offshore winds blowing in
the movement of leaves in the forest and you know
what night occludes doesn't cease
for lack of seeing and all that there is
is only ahead or behind
a central position

                        an empty chair facing east
(details he labours as smudges and drips decorate his limbs)
before he wakes he paints a fire close to keep his son warm

    *

CONVERGENCE

on the headland two forms face
they shape from the rock itself

in intimate recline a landscape falls
its air its water its rock

clouds scud and tumble the sun
each shade each texture

in this progression of light
every change every weather

the way sound carries through winter
art makes clear

Louise Waller

Four Ways to Approach the Numinous

I. BY THE MYSTERY OF PRESENCE

Gabrielle d'Estrées and one of her sisters, both naked
Are standing in what might be a bath. Lining its sides
Are milk coffee cloths, gathered and pleated by water.
Upstage in the gloom a fully clothed woman is sewing.

On each side a red satin curtain is tied back
Allowing the viewer a clear frontal view of the two sisters,
Who seem expressionless or, to be perhaps more precise,
Are giving nothing away because the pressure of decorum

Requires them to restrain, contain but nevertheless be aware
Of a considerable cargo of physical and metaphysical truths.
Above the woman sewing is the lower half of a painting
Of male legs suggesting a depleted Mars in disarray.

But the sisters' reticence and a mysterious and pervasive air,
As if they breathed pure nitrogen, makes instances of symbolism
Difficult to identify. One sister holds a pale nipple of the other
Between thumb and index finger in a circle, the hand highly

Stylised like a Balinese dancer's. The other holds a ring,
Her own hand forming a second, almost identical circle.
Their four forearms make a separate formal geometry,
As if this tableau of arms in itself represented something

Like an epigram the viewer should be able to read but cannot.
Their breasts, which lie in a single horizontal line,
Are small, conical and, as it were, undemonstrative,
Like four mounds in a raked Zen garden.

It is as if time had stopped several minutes earlier – perhaps
At the moment the one reached out her right hand
To the other's breast. It appears, although this may seem fanciful,
That she is adjusting the vertical hold in some sixteenth century

Equivalent of a screen bombarded from behind by electrons
So as to achieve an unstable, shuddering stillness
In which nothing else other than this gesture is happening
And the viewer watches some unchanging studio test-pattern.

Two pearl drop-earrings are visible, one obscured on each sister
By their centralising gaze. An unsatisfactory permanence
Seems to exclude the possibility of any future action
Such as stepping from the bath or drying or smiling.

II. BY EMBRACING MULTIPLICITY

Seven roads diverge in a wood
And at their point of departure
An acolyte meets a Master and asks him, 'Master!
How should I decide which path to take?
I know that at the end of one is a voluptuous tavern;
Another contains a cinema of dreams; a third
Offers cyber-space access to the past;
Another has a coin-in-the-slot peep-show
Of selected future events which, it is said,
Is fully interactive; another leads to the sea
With hire-boats and a favourable breeze waiting;
Another leads to a pavilion in which there are
Extensive and documented views of this very place of departure;
Another leads through a wilderness which is constantly changing
So that none can predict for a moment
The experience which might be gained there –'

The Master replies. 'I know you too well. You ask me this
Expecting me to answer in an enigma or reversal
Of all your expectations of an answer, or propose
Staying very still here at this point of indecision
So that all seven roads flow gently back to you,
Or give you a method of visiting all at once,
Even perhaps pointing you (in the Borgesian use
Of the term) to an Aleph where All is One
And where the angels put on a large dance-fest
In a ballroom on the head of a pin – and you're invited.
Perhaps you half expect me to announce steps
Leading underground which circumvent all seven paths,
Or conversely ease you into the gondola of a balloon
In which you might rise serenely into the air
To let the winds take you everywhere and anywhere –
But you have become too dependent on such contractions.
You have relied too long on everything approaching you
In labelled clusters or packets or quanta.
You have become accustomed to assuming the atoms
Of events may be combined into the molecules
Of experience, and this is not necessarily so.
You view everything as problem and seek a solution.
You expect that from every diverging path
There will be bridges to others, and this also
Is not necessarily so. I could continue, pointing out
Other radical simplifications you have unwittingly – Ah!'
The Master observes that his words are having
The desired effect: the acolyte's head is nodding
With weariness at so many words of reply; he leans
Against the broken and loosely turning signpost.
And soon the Master notes with satisfaction
(To a degree not incompatible with his humility as Master)
That the acolyte has fallen into a peaceful sleep.

III. By a Devotion to Objects

Morandi crossed the borders of Italy into the wide world
Twice only, and one of these occasions was to see
Paintings on the shores of a Swiss-Italian lake.
Otherwise he was frequently in his room allowing
His thoughts to gather dust and eliminate glare.

It is pleasing to imagine oneself actually standing
In that room (a bedroom) in front of a table
On which the votive objects stand. And to see oneself
Seeing them, like tourists in Rome for the Tiber spring flood,
Or viewing the Eiffel Tower with some degree of dispassion.

The objects are a group of bottles or canisters
Or ointment jars standing on a shelf
Crowding together like cows in a field, lowing,
Lowering their gaze, looking up, chewing cud,
Staring curiously behind a simple wire fence.

The still lifes made from this array are as familiar
As a coat hanging in a hall, and one need remark merely
On the propensity for that frieze of containers
To discourage, deny, descry any implication
That they contain anything at all, or that

They were assembled to assert in any way
Anything symbolic, allusive, shamanistic, allegorical,
Even nostalgic or tinged with sadness. Rather
It would appear they have arrived, jostled slightly
Then settled to attempt to profess essence merely.

Similarly one might consider one of several
Outdoor scenes. For instance here is something close
To a square representing the side of a house
Bordered by a dissemblance of trees like hair
And what looks like a trapezoid of ploughed ground,

That wall windowless, a churned-ricotta-white
With the tree backing off lest its shadow
Assume greater moment than its canopied branch.
Some claw marks partly distinguish the wall
From a rhombus of brown-purple (a field).

So reticent are these shaded areas with shadows
Posited in the gestures of eucalypt or conifer
One might well be in the afternoon lace-cloth interior
Of the room in its Bolognese cool with the footfalls
Of three sisters elsewhere in the echoing house.

One would like to press further into this sub-tropical, leafy
Interior, this haven of shadows, and ask the reader
Stationed as he is at the apex of a triangle
Whose other vertices are these meditations and Morandi's
    tableau,
To allow these two to overlap and coalesce further,

As the eyes focussing after a reverie recombine
Two adjacencies into a single and singular éclat,
With the clarity of the gaze from a window
At the unflinching presence of umbrella pines like clouds
On an autumn afternoon in a rising breeze.

IV. By Approaching the River

Towards the general wellspring of recollection itself
An instinctive resistance to being drawn surfaced, as if,
Once on display there, all original impulses must fail;

Or perhaps there was a desire to prevent the fall,
Into the general wellspring of recollection itself,
Of the floating world which so innocently, so vulnerably,

Was passing, intact and entire and magisterial:
The river surface, for instance, like a titanium mirror
Undisturbed, impossibly large, where siftings of rain already fell,

And a pelican single and solitary was indecisive about
Arrival and take-off with a little track of wake
Attesting to the intermittence of its resolve – O

How the general wellspring of recollection itself
Wants to take such epiphanies from the bystander
But does so peremptorily, is careless in taking

The choicest fruit from the centre of the pyramid,
So that the edifice pauses before collapsing suddenly
And spills out over the surrounding lawns,

Out of the general wellspring of recollection itself
And into the increasing disorder of Lost Property
Where float worlds of simulacra and dockets and motes.

But to the river! whose two divulged items, bird and rain,
Were tiny portions of an indivisible and larger whole:
These now threaten to overturn their floundering vessel,

For being singled out inevitably ties weights to the rest
And throws them overboard in a tangle of floating and sinking.
The boat rocks dangerously. And yet of course

There was no boat to be seen on the original river, nothing
So graspable or large. For some minutes before the first
Drops of rain the Gesualdo madrigals veered and tangled

Of crows somewhere invisible amongst trees on the opposite
    bank;
The wrens' tiny flit and flight amongst aniseed trees,
A heron flying overhead just when items of similar degrees

Of granulation seemed to have been skimmed cleanly
From the surface of the eventful world; shimmers where
A fish may or may not have leapt, circles fading

Like the general wellspring of recollection itself,
And reflections – most ambiguously falling between
Incident and steady state – reflections of hinterland

Lowered in competing layers and of the blue torn openings
Between clouds, a stronger blue as reflections than above them.
And sounds! On the one hand the sound of grass

Being twisted then torn by a cow's tongue
Just behind the matted fence, and, on the other,
The sound like an improvisation for pins and pincushions

Of the rain falling lightly across the whole water sheet.
With the thought that exhaustive description may render
    appearances
Less susceptible to being made metaphor, the river divulges

Incident after incident: the stained grey tarpaulin looses
Tiny spiralling orbits, leaves moving in a slow convoy, aggregates
Of pollen; and the river announces a momentous event:

It is quasi-noon. The slow drift of tidal water
Hesitates, about to change direction, as if to reverse
The general wellspring of recollection itself.

John Watson

Holbein Through Silk

Death, the cool, black ambassadress, is foetal, rigor,
silk in that rough skull's glass mouth.
Death, she sits, the foliate weave of her fingers
is their tender matrix. The intuitive, the profane,
the incalculable, the vernal seat, indulged. Death,
the echolalic, the echopractic. Death,
the parrot, the mirror of men. Death,
Holbein's electric squirrel on a chain,
the voltage of its bondage readable,
tail bristling, its free foil, a bird with patina,
leans to speak. Death, the white stubble
on Sir Thomas More's chin. Death,
the lit creases in his velvet sleeves. Death,
the gold, the impotent fur that covers his skin
with prurience. Death, his bright body. Death,
in family portraits. Tightly plaited into daughters'
thin hair. Death, first wives, children. Death, tendrils,
sprigs in bodices, stiffened voile. Death,
ornamental pillars. Death, open-mouthed faces
hung by the hair. Death, in each embroidered stitch,
in each royal ring, in each eye, in each ear,
each pearl a death. Death in each twisted, fastening cord
tied by a dresser, in each chain, each pendant,
each beard combed by a dresser, the king placid, dressed.
Death, in inanimate things. Death, the oak for panels
and brushes. Death, chalked, washed paper. Death,
plucked fur spiked with paint. Death in pigments,
lakes, lead, rosin, linseed, tung, turpentine. Death,
organic death. Death, Holbein's father, Holbein's son.
Death in 1533 to the Incas. Death, Elizabeth I born.
Death, the cool, black ambassadress (whispers through silk).

Meredith Wattison

Dysfunction, North Carlton Style or The Widow of Noosa

for Mark 'The Kevin Spacey of Lygon Street' Rubbo

I'd love you to meet this exemplary couple,
swinging and sexy and very well liked.
Here in a suburb where values quintuple
over thirty-plus years and they still haven't spiked.

Our lucky two bathed in gold adulations
(golden as sun-ripened corn on the cob)
poets would offer them book dedications:
For North Carlton's finest, Ali and Bob.

Both won medals when they obtained their degrees,
they seemed immune to the snigger and scoff.
Their boys' names arose out of excellent pedigrees:
Dustin from Hoffman and Gough after Gough.

Allison, Robert held drink-till-you-burst nights,
both played around although both returned home.
Footy 'n' demos 'n' La Mama first nights,
you do, as the cliché says, when you're in Rome.

An architect, Bob possessed mighty dimensions:
a proud blooming afro, a grand frontal lobe.
He designed half of North Carlton's extensions.
She lectured in ethics, out at La Trobe.

Long-haired, even-featured, an absolute Ali
(is it any wonder she looked like McGraw?).
On their sun deck each summer how Bob's loins would rally
at the sight of his missus, spread out in the raw.

Their pleasuring rated A plus (and I kid not).
When the urge turned to threesomes though Ali got stoned.
It sort of worked once but most times it did not,
such acts seemed mechanical, non-comfort-zoned.

Sure Ali was patient with Bob's peccadillos,
she thought them, and then turned explosive in bed,
and uttered, as they stared from opposite pillows
these very first words coming into her head:

'Two decades of marriage,' (that sounded amazing!)
'and a girl gets, well, notions as she starts to slow.
You're my main repast so I'll only be grazing,
but I'm after the Big One, Bob, I have to *know*.'

'Please hunt out amours whilst your spouse remains maison'd
there's Eddie, there's Freddie, there's Gilbert 'n' Gabe …'
On Bob's beaming grin these words seemed emblazoned:
If Baby Feels Happy I'm Happy For Babe.

Ali mused to herself: 'You've just crossed that first bridge.'
The second and third proved far more than she hoped.
For Tristram was chosen, the satyr of Hurstbridge,
the full sexist boor, how he ogled and groped.

Not that his body was flaccid or putrid,
his gifts were delivered with heft of an axe.
Never before was she *this* Kama Sutra'd,
so home the wife drove to deliver the facts.

'Mon-Tues-Wed-Thurs-Fri, whatever the day be
I'm here ...' her man bleated. She felt like a grub.
'But weekends are my times for lovin' you Baby ...
yeah well see you later I'm off to the pub.'

Bob's mates were protective, they counselled 'Quit mopin''
so the pendulum swung back to full raging shock:
'If our marriage is open I don't mean *this* open,
I can't stand that deadshit, his brains or his cock!'

Whole blocks caught the grind of this marital mincer
with its venomous churn through the four a.m. peace,
requiring a movement, which movement turned pincer
as neighbours on all sides called forth the police.

In the wagon they both cried, 'It's off to the piggery!
Who'll bail us out? Let's ask Dustin and Gough.
What a fine place to perform jiggy-jiggery!'
And that's where the cops found 'em, gettin' it off.

Dustin kept sneering, 'Go suck a tablet.'
Gough hectored and lectured as each hung their head:
'You embarrass us more than a Carey or Ablett.
We put you on notice. Now go to your bed!'

Dustin was criminal (no need to hide it)
he skirted those haunts where the Carlton Crew thrive.
You name the drug the lad probably tried it,
he was pockmarked and sallow, and yet still alive.

'I'll turn out,' Gough fancied, 'an ace merchant banker
and when politics beckons I'll run for the Libs!'
'Dumb cunt,' his dad grunted, 'smart arse, yuppie wanker.'
Mum's mode was more pre-school: 'Now stop telling fibs.'

And for solacing tracks Ali put on The Seekers
whilst later, by contrast, Bob grooved to The Fugs.
So their boys became two motivational speakers,
what self-gratifyingly filial-thugs:

'From now on we're nuking,' they bellowed, 'these tumours.
For two lifetimes long we've a-hummed and a-hemmed.
You know the rumours, our parents are 'boomers,
both fatuous phonies and THEY ARE CONDEMNED!'

Was this the result of his sons' condemnation:
their father recoiling 'What, *moi* undersexed?'
But the quack with his monotone bedside oration
told something had blossomed. And Robert was hexed.

For the whole universe was chomping his prostate,
'And Babe here's' he told her, 'the aspect that galls:
why in the past day of kilos I've lost eight?
'cause adios comrade, it's gone to me balls!'

Just after Lorne they would bury his ashes
with sighs to the elements, muses and fates.
There were painters and punters and dopeheads with stashes,
three current lovers and unending mates.

There was Jimmo and Timmo and Kimmo and Simmo
plying the widow with grief overload.
Gough hadn't hired he had *bought* a stretch limo,
and thus they returned up the Great Ocean Road.

*

Control-freaking Dustin's a prime mega-locust,
there in his penthouse he peddles his ice.
When you're this dealer y'gotta be focused
(each year he remembers mum, at the most twice).

'Father, that dickhead, thought I was bluffing.
North Carlton?' Gough sneers, 'What an out 'n' out hole.'
From his Double Bay villa behold it is nothing
jetting in Gran for her babysit role.

And needing at this time no bloke to seduce her
(though options stay open, we'll see where that ends)
Ali's turned into the Widow of Noosa
with her new and evolving collection of friends.

Like this Ozlit emeritus calling her 'Matey',
as their reading group ploughs on through trash and through
    bard.
She sure brings the best out in chaps over eighty,
whilst he swaps his Tranter for her Kierkegaard.

Or that cutesy barista who blurts without stalling:
'You're *what* side of sixty? Geez y'look grouse.'
Making Allison's day as she spends it recalling
how she rooted North Carlton, though mostly her spouse.

Alan Wearne

The Orchardist

Renmark, South Australia (Riverland)

In the bitten dusk, his lemons
gleamed their own light, too much, too rich for harvest.
He was blacklisted, we later learned, for cheating workers,
the wretched flesh, unpredictable as weather,
he hated to need. Two kids aged 9 and 10 had spidered
words in Romanian on the bedroom wall
in the derelict fruitpickers' house.

At night we walked the river, following its curves
that wound us out to where a redgum
stood marooned at water's edge, fossilised in thirst;
a sliver of silver still flashing
in the cavernous bed, eluding, for now,
the underground stealthwork of pipes tugging the river
out of itself, into the ticking sprinklers.

At dawn we were into the fragrant avenues of citrus,
dreamily caught in the strangeness of labour.
Throwing our ladders on the mass of a laden tree,
lunging blind into the leaves, we learned
by hand instead of heart; our finger-muscles
rippling up, reaching and grabbing, tearing the fruit
from its branch as if from a painting.

All day the farmer circled on his tractor, mad as a bull-rider,
lurching on thick dry mud-tracks braided yesterday
and yesterday, shouting *Truck coming tomorrow!*
as if to say, *The end of the world!* On our last day
his neighbours mushroomed in the avenues
to help; sauntering past us, he glinted in defiance: *I hire
a million dollars and grow this up from nothing!*

Petra White

Kinglake

for Chewy and Ella

1.
Short glass, the petrol gleam
      of the dark liquid. Expecting still
the black print of his fingers on its rim.

The terrible currency of searching –
his hands collect the downy weight of ash
and heavy emptiness

as others filled
with scattered teeth and jewellery.
Boiled flesh within water tanks.
White helmet. Monkey bars.

The smoke ghosts the rest of his platoon,
their limbs long and black. A silence
eucalypt and lunar.

2.
How a burning piano must sing.
The years of oil on the cold keys
from your fingers' skin
mellowing the timbre.

The full-throated tenor of the flame,
the crackling wood, the sharpened ping
        of each string's tight, tuned snap.

Exploding eucalypts will echo in your chest
        years later.

Your orchard eaten into black dust.
I send you irises,
        and try to write
some kind of greening.

Fiona Wright

Pages

after Cavafy

Sitting late into the night,
cluttered table, old books,
clumsy commentaries on long-
forgotten texts, a lost world in my head.
My life as full of names
as an abandoned cemetery or
phone book in a foreign city,
the city of my ancestors.

See where it stands, so glossy,
vibrant, new, a lure for export only.

I stare at a half-finished loose iambic
mix, formal twinned with the vernacular,
pushing up from some lost seedbed
where the roots began: parents who loved
me, suffered big words from an unfledged beak,
friends dead, lost or mad, private mirage of
solace looming, vanishing.

Were summer evenings ever so alive with birds?
So tranquil? Was the sky that blue?
Who really lived there?

The barbarians have taken my city,
its citizens barnacled to ancient rites.

The homeland trap: huge silences
over dark bluestone streets once
sites of transgression, the wrong company.
Done in by dangerous allure, I flew the coop,
letting fly to learn by leaving
what I knew, grow old imagining.

A woman with a notebook in her hand
turning pages like wings.

Fay Zwicky

Publication Details

Adam Aitken's 'Pol Pot in Paris' appeared in *Jacket 36*, 2008.

Ivy Alvarez's 'Curing the animal' appeared in *Cordite 29: Pastoral*, 2008.

Mandy Beaumont's 'We Are Standing' was previously unpublished.

Sarak K. Bell's 'reconstructing a rabbit' appeared in *Cordite 30: Custom/Made*, 2009.

Judith Beveridge's 'Rain' appeared in *Australian Book Review*, June 2009, and in her collection, *Storm and Honey*, Giramondo Publishing, 2009.

Judith Bishop's 'In the Somme' was previously unpublished.

Ken Bolton's '*Outdoor Pig-Keeping*, 1954 & My Other Books on Farming Pigs' appeared in *HEAT 21: Without a Paddle*, 2009.

Michael Brennan's 'After Fred Williams' *You Yangs 1*' was written for *Poets Paint Words II* in Newcastle as part of the Sydney Writers' Festival, 2009.

David Brooks' 'A Place on Earth' appeared in *Meanjin*, Vol. 67, No. 4, 2008; '*Ninox strenua*' was previously unpublished.

Jen Jewel Brown's 'breath' appeared in *Cordite 29: Pastoral*, 2008.

Pam Brown's 'Blue Glow' was previously unpublished.

joanne burns' 'harbinger' appeared in *Conversations from the Bottom of the Harbour*, Harbour City Poets chapbook, Puncher & Wattman, May 2009.

Larry Buttrose's 'London Fields' was previously unpublished.

Michelle Cahill's 'After the Headlines' appeared in *The Age*, 30 May 2009.

Elizabeth Campbell's 'Ithaka' appeared in the *Australian Literary Review*, October 2009.

Ali Cobby Eckermann's 'Intervention Pay Back' appeared in the Northern Territory Literary Awards 2008 anthology and *Fishtails in the Dust: Writing from the Centre*, Ed. Janet Huchinson, Ptilotus Press, 2009.

Stuart Cooke's 'North Durras Caravan Park' was previously unpublished.

Shevaun Cooley's 'Expeditions with W.G. Sebald' appeared in *To Sculpt the Moment: Newcastle Poetry Prize 2008*, Ed. Jan Owen, Hunter Writers' Centre, 2008.

Luke Davies' 'Maldon, 991 A.D.' appeared online in *Snorkel # 8*, October 2008.

Sarah Day's 'A Dry Winter: Some Observations About Rain' appeared in *The Age*, 30 May 2009, and in her collection, *Grass Notes*, Brandl & Schlesinger, 2009.

Lucy Dougan's 'The Ties My Sister Makes' was previously unpublished.

Laurie Duggan's 'Letter to John Forbes' was previously unpublished.

Adrienne Eberhard's 'The Maze' appeared in *Meanjin*, Vol. 68, No. 1, 2009, and in *Take Five*, Ed. Adrian Caesar, Shoestring Press, Nottingham (UK), 2009.

Stephen Edgar's 'Murray Dreaming' appeared in *Poetry* Chicago, November 2008, and *Island* 115, April 2009.

Chris Edwards' 'The Big Splash' appeared online in *Stylus Poetry Journal*, Issue 34, July 2009.

Anne Elvey's 'Between' appeared in *Cordite 30: Custom/Made*, 2009.

Kate Fagan's 'From *The Correspondence*' (Letter VI) appeared in the US journal *Ecopoetics*, Volumes 6/7, 2009; Letters IV and VII were previously unpublished.

Jeltje Fanoy's 'Surfers Paradise (Qld)/Reporting for the Night Watch' was previously unpublished.

Michael Farrell's 'muzak to view the city with' appeared in *The Age*, 21 February 2009.

Susan Fealy's 'Notes on Art and Dying: 19.10.2008 ... *How to paint a rose*' appeared online in *The Merri Creek: Poems and Pieces # 9*, Collected Works – Poetry & Ideas blogspot, February 2009.

Johanna Featherstone's 'Mother Looking into Her Son's Bedroom' was previously unpublished.

Jayne Fenton Keane's 'The Boot Left in the Snow' formed part of the script for 'Dive', broadcast for ABC Radio National's *A Pod of Poets*.

Clare Gaskin's 'Exile' was previously unpublished.

Jane Gibian's 'Sound Piece' appeared in *Meanjin*, Vol. 68, No. 2, 2009.

Lisa Gorton's 'A Description of the Storm Glass and Guide to Its Use in Forecasting Weather' (Part 1) appeared in an earlier version in *The Age*, 14 June 2008; an earlier version of Parts 2 and 3 appeared in *Australian Book Review*, March 2009.

Robert Gray's 'Classifying the Animals' appeared in *The Write Stuff*, Northern Rivers Writers' Centre, July–August 2009.

Jennifer Harrison's 'Kakadu' appeared in *Perihelion Review* (USA), www.perihelionreview.com.

Martin Harrison's 'Word' was previously unpublished; 'Wallabies' appeared in *Poetry Review* (UK), Vol. 99, No. 1, 2009.

J.S. Harry's 'Braid on Braid' appeared in *HEAT 18: The Library of Fire*, 2008.

Kevin Hart's 'Dark Bird' will appear in a forthcoming issue of *Virginia Quarterly Review* (USA).

Susan Hawthorne's 'Climate change: *yugantameghaha*' appeared in *The Age*, 11 October 2008, and in her collection, *Earth's Breath*, Spinifex Press, 2009.

Matt Hetherington's 'The words in brackets are from Gaskin's "A Bud"' was previously unpublished.

Barry Hill's 'Egret' and 'Waking Happens in Reservoirs' appeared in *Four Lines East*, Whitmore Press, 2009.

Lia Hills' 'an anatomy of birds' appeared online in *foam:e*, Issue 5, 2008, and in her collection, *the possibility of flight*, Interactive Press, 2008.

Sarah Holland-Batt's 'Capriccio: Spring' appeared in *HEAT 20: Plain Vanilla Futures*, 2009.

L.K. Holt's 'For Nina' was previously unpublished.

Clive James' '*Meteor IV* at Cowes, 1913' appeared in *Meanjin*, Vol. 68, No. 1, 2009.

Carol Jenkins' 'When Years Take the Stars Away' appeared in her collection, *Fishing in the Devonian*, Puncher & Wattmann, 2008.

A. Frances Johnson's 'Black Cockatoo: *Calyptorhynchus funereus*' and 'The Wind-up Birdman of Moorabool Street' were previously unpublished.

Jill Jones' 'Oh, Sydney' appeared in the *Australian Literary Review*, March 2009.

Amanda Joy's 'Chased Seas Urge' appeared in *SpeedPoets*, Vol. 8, No. 1, February 2009.

Paul Kelly's 'Thoughts in the Middle of the Night' appeared on his album *Songs From The South Vol. 2*; 'One More Tune' has been performed live but is yet to be recorded.

Anthony Lawrence's 'Leonard Cohen in Concert, Hunter Valley, January 2009' and 'The Burden & the Wing' were previously unpublished.

Michelle Leber's 'Heat Wave, Melbourne' appeared in *Meanjin*, Vol. 68, No. 3, 2009.

Geoffrey Lehmann's 'The Animals' appeared in *The New Yorker*, 1 June 2009.

John Leonard's 'Rain in March' was previously unpublished.

Kerry Leves' '"We believe in killing idiots"' was previously unpublished.

Debbie Lim's 'The Egret' was previously unpublished.

Astrid Lorange's 'Fred's Farm' was previously unpublished.

Rose Lucas' 'Even in the Dark' appeared in *Meanjin*, Vol. 68, No. 2, 2009.

Kent MacCarter's 'Twenty-five Unbroken Bottles of Champ' appeared in *Westerly*, Vol. 53, 2008, and in his collection, *In the Middle of Here*, Transit Lounge, 2009.

Jennifer Maiden's 'Clare and Paris' appeared in *HEAT 20: Plain Vanilla Futures*, 2009.

David McCooey's 'Memory & Slaughter' was previously unpublished.

Susan McCreery's 'Rock Fishing' appeared in *Poetrix*, No. 32, May 2009.

Kate Middleton's 'To Peter Rabbit in the Night' was previously unpublished.

Peter Minter's 'The Latter Shall Prevail' was previously unpublished.

Meg Mooney's 'Birdwatching during the Intervention' appeared in *Fishtails in the Dust: Writing from the Centre*, Ed. Janet Huchinson, Ptilotus Press, 2009.

Derek Motion's 'hush' appeared in *The Age*, 23 May 2009.

Les Murray's 'Port Jackson Greaseproof Rose' appeared in *Quadrant*, Vol. LIII, No. 5, May 2009.

David Musgrave's 'Phantom Limb' appeared in *Crannóg* literary magazine (Ireland), Vol. 17, Spring 2008.

Jenni Nixon's 'A Bombardier on the Bus' appeared in *Conversations from the Bottom of the Harbour*, Harbour City Poets chapbook,

Puncher & Wattman, May 2009, and in her collection, *Agenda!*, Picaro Press, 2009.

Jan Owen's 'Climbing the Nectarine Tree at Dusk' appeared in *Take Five*, Ed. Adrian Caesar, Shoestring Press, Nottingham (UK), 2009.

Geoff Page's 'Richard Rorty (1931–2007)' appeared in *HEAT 19: Trappers Way*, 2009.

π.O.'s '"Mo" McCackie 1892–1953' appeared in *Meanjin*, Vol. 67, No. 4, 2008.

Felicity Plunkett's 'Venery' appeared in the *Australian Literary Review*, June 2009, and in her collection, *Vanishing Point*, UQP, 2009.

Dorothy Porter's 'Travel' appeared in *Australian Book Review*, January 2009, and in her collection, *The Bee Hut*, Black Inc., 2009.

Peter Porter's 'After Schiller' was previously unpublished.

Ron Pretty's 'Kate Dancing' appeared in *Westerly*, Vol. 53, 2008.

Peter Rose's 'Morbid Transfers' appeared in the *Australian Literary Review*, November 2009.

Robyn Rowland's 'Is the light right?' was previously unpublished.

Gig Ryan's 'Tormented Syllogism Held at Bay' was previously unpublished.

Philip Salom's 'Reading Francis Webb' was previously unpublished.

Jaya Savige's 'The Pain Switch' appeared in *The Age*, 26 April 2008.

Berndt Sellheim's 'Necromantic' was previously unpublished.

Thomas Shapcott's 'Monteverdi at 74' appeared in *HEAT 18: The Library of Fire*, 2008.

Craig Sherborne's 'Slipper' appeared in *The Age*, 7 February 2009.

Alex Skovron's 'Lives' was previously unpublished.

Andrew Slattery's 'Triptych' appeared in his collection, *Canyon*, The Australian Poetry Centre, 2009.

Vivian Smith's 'In the Butterfly House, Vienna' appeared in *HEAT 18: The Library of Fire*, 2008.

Alicia Sometimes' 'This Machine Kills Fascists' appeared in *fourW: Nineteen*, November 2008.

Maria Takolander's 'Anaesthetic' appeared in *Island* 118, October 2009.

Tim Thorne's 'Cimitière Marin Revisited' appeared in *HEAT 19: Trappers Way*, 2009.

Jessika Tong's 'The Light Went Off in Me' appeared in the *Australian Literary Review*, December 2008, and in her collection *The Anatomy of Blue*, SunLine Press, 2008.

John Tranter's 'The Anaglyph' appeared in the *Australian Literary Review*, May 2009.

Mark Tredinnick's 'Improvisations on a Daylight Moon' appeared in *Meanjin*, Vol. 67, No. 4, 2008, and in his collection, *The Road South*, River Road Press, 2008.

Chris Wallace-Crabbe's 'Torture is a Dirty Word' appeared online in *Eureka Street*, Vol. 19, No. 11, June 2009.

Louise Waller's 'Three Rivers Triptych' appeared online in *foam:e*, Issue 6, 2009.

John Watson's 'Four Ways to Approach the Numinous' is the previously unpublished recipient of the 2009 Blake Poetry Prize.

Meredith Wattison's 'Holbein Through Silk' appeared in *Meanjin*, Vol. 67, No. 4, 2008.

Alan Wearne's 'Dysfunction, North Carlton Style or The Widow of Noosa' appeared in *HEAT 20: Plain Vanilla Futures*, 2009.

Petra White's 'The Orchardist' appeared in an earlier version in *fourW: Nineteen*, November 2008.

Fiona Wright's 'Kinglake' appeared in the *Australian Literary Review*, July 2009.

Fay Zwicky's 'Pages' appeared in *HEAT 18: The Library of Fire*, 2008.